Stephanie Lovegrove is a barrister at 4-5 Gray's Inn Square specialising in Housing, Landlord and Tenant and related Local Government and Property law. She has over 19 years of experience acting for and advising both landlords and tenants in housing-related matters, including succession-related policy development, procedures and possession claims.

Stephanie is ranked in both Chambers and Partners and the Legal 500 where she has been described as "demonstrating prowess across all areas of landlord and tenant law", "absolutely excellent: clients and solicitors love her alike", and it said that "her intelligence and her knowledge of housing law will blow anyone away".

A Practical Guide to Succession to Social Housing Tenancies

A Practical Guide to Succession to Social Housing Tenancies

Stephanie Lovegrove

BA Hons (Oxon)

Barrister at Law, 4-5 Gray's Inn Square (London),

Housing, Local Government, Property

Law Brief Publishing

Published 2023 by Law Brief Publishing, an imprint of Law Brief Publishing Ltd
30 The Parks
Minehead
Somerset
TA24 8BT

www.lawbriefpublishing.com

Paperback: 978-1-914608-37-7

For Alexandra

PREFACE

The law of succession to social housing tenancies is complex and fact sensitive. The tenancies at stake are valuable to potential successors both financially and for their ability to provide family stability and community coherence. For landlords, the drive to identify and free up accommodation to support local authorities in the discharge of their homelessness and housing functions has arguably never been more necessary.

Whilst there are exceptional specialist firms of solicitors (and law centres) out there which deal with tenancy succession-related advice and litigation, the difficulty many potential successors face is that such advice is no longer local to them. A person's instinct will be to approach local law firms for assistance. One of the aims of this book is to provide the lawyers who work in those firms and law centres with the tools needed to give advice quickly and manage litigation effectively.

Thanks go to Tim Kevan for yet another opportunity to write for the masses and to Garry Wright for his Herculean patience and understanding.

I also give thanks to my family: my parents and stepparents for their unwavering support and generosity; my brother for his hilarious yet mocking memes; and my daughter who has (since my last book) jettisoned Nerf guns and decided that mum writing means she can develop her Tik Tok dance moves.

Finally, I give my thanks to Emily Martin and the clerking team at 4-5 Gray's Inn Square who remind me I *can* do hard things well.

The law is accurate as of 1 January 2023.

Stephanie Lovegrove
January 2023

CONTENTS

CHAPTER ONE

INTRODUCTION

What is tenancy succession? Broadly, it is what happens when a tenant dies and there is in existence a legal right for someone else (potentially one of a number of others) to take over their tenancy and become the tenant of the same property. It is the legal process by which someone steps into the deceased tenant's shoes. All the rights (and, yes, liabilities) of the deceased tenant in relation to the tenancy become those of the "successor" tenant, including where applicable, the right to buy, the payment of rent and any arrears, using the property in a tenant-like manner, not causing nuisance and so on.

It will be apparent that there are considerable benefits to those who are entitled to succeed in exercising their right to do so. Likewise, there can be considerable advantages to a social landlord, where a tenant has died and leaves a property under-occupied, in taking the property back into their stock and allocating it to a suitably sized family on their housing waiting list.

And so, to an extent, the scene for what follows is set.

This book provides (from a client-neutral perspective) a practical guide to navigating the area of succession to social housing tenancies for legal advisors, officers in local government, employees in housing associations and other registered providers of social housing and potential successors.

In this author's view, it is a fascinating area for those who love overlapping areas of law: you have a wonderful mixture of landlord and tenant law, social housing law, wills and probate, intestacy and trusts. However, the resultant complexity can lead to unexpected outcomes and there are fair-few pitfalls for practitioners, from accidentally granting new tenancies, through conferring or missing out on succession rights, and ending with unsuccessful possession proceedings e.g., because a succession policy has been overlooked or applied incorrectly.

I made the point in the introductory chapter to "A Practical Guide to the Law of Unlawful Eviction and Harassment", Law Brief Publishing (2020) that the value of a person's home cannot be overstated: that it is a place of sanctuary, privacy, comfort and enjoyment. In context, I can add that it is also where families are raised, memories are made, and communities forged. Its value to a potential successor goes beyond the expense and inconvenience of securing alternative accommodation in the private sector, and emotions and passions can often run high in the event of litigation.

At a basic level, the difficulty faced by successive governments – arising from the social housing model adopted in this country – has been balancing the competing objectives of (i) securing longer-term accommodation which gives individuals and families (particularly children) stable and suitably-sized homes from which to build (hopefully) successful lives and communities; and (ii) freeing up enough suitably sized accommodation in the social rented sector to provide for those most in need of it.

The situation in England now is very different to what it once was: with pressures on local authority and registered providers of social housing stock at (or beyond) bursting point, it is unsurprising that statutory requirements relating to succession have been tightened (by the Localism Act 2012) yet social landlords now have far greater say over how the balance between building communities and making stock available is struck. This change has not been adopted in Wales despite the long-awaited introduction of the Renting Homes (Wales) Act 2016 ("RH(W) Act 2016") which came into force on 1 December 2022 where a more generous and generic approach has been taken than that in England.

So, what of all this for practitioners?

With the background described above, it is apparent that litigation is at the least to be anticipated when the issue of (particularly intergenerational) succession arises. Whether you are a provider of social housing (including a local authority), a potential successor or an advisor of either, the need to record and have regard to the following should be apparent:

- the nature and terms of the applicable tenancy agreement (including any transfers, assignments and/or variations),

- any applicable policies and practices (these appear second in the list for a reason – it informs the scope of the right to succeed and too often is considered last and least),

- relevant legislation (ordinarily in England the Housing Acts of 1985, 1988 and 1996 (all as amended by the Localism Act 2012 and RH(W) Act 2016 in Wales),

- proof of the tenant's death (and if formerly a joint tenant, the deceased joint tenant's death),

- proof of relationship (marriage/birth etc.),

- detailed records showing occupation of the property over time (usually but not invariably the 12 months immediately before death as a minimum).

This is a practitioner's starting point. From the above documents and information, a case on succession can begin to be built.

So let construction commence…

CHAPTER TWO

WHAT IS TENANCY SUCCESSION?

We touched upon it in the introduction in brief terms. Essentially, succession to a tenancy is the process by which a tenancy passes on the death of the tenant to a person "qualified to succeed" to it. Sometimes, that person is selected by the tenant (e.g., in their will) or the person succeeds automatically under a statutory provision (for example if they lived with the tenant for a period of time before their death and they are a qualifying family member) or the landlord has chosen who is entitled to succeed in the terms and conditions of the tenancy agreement signed by the original tenant.

We will look at the specific methods by which succession to certain types of social housing tenancies happens in later chapters.

This chapter is concerned with the "nuts and bolts" of the law of estates, wills and intestacy which dictate what happens to a tenancy on death. It's not an easy (or even settled!) area of law, but you need to understand it to be able to grapple with the technical aspects of a succession case. It is the "bedrock" on which contractual and statutory succession to social housing tenancies is built in England (and was – until recently – in Wales).

What happens to a tenancy when the tenant dies?

We are not concerned with tenancies at will in this book (which is helpful because the law is different concerning what happens on death with those types of tenancy). For any other tenancy (by which we mean exclusive occupation of defined land/property granted for a term of years – in context – for a rent) on the death of the tenant, the tenancy does not come to an end (the technical term for which is "determine" which I will use throughout this book).

But why does it not determine? Surely, if there is no tenant, there cannot be a tenancy? The starting point is in the nature of tenancies. They arise by contract (a grant of tenancy) and the contract (at least initially) governs the terms of the tenancy but the tenancy itself is an "estate in land" – it is a form of tenure (how land is held or owned) carved out of another larger form of tenure (so, a freehold owner might – by contract – carve out a time-limited portion of his freehold by way of a lease of say 999 years; in turn that leasehold owner can carve out a smaller form of tenure in a 125-year lease and so on). The point we take from this is that a tenant is not merely a person who agrees to occupy land belonging to another, but in fact (in the case of a legal tenancy) holds a time-limited part of the freehold, a term of years absolute, or a lease/tenancy which is itself one of only two legally recognised estates in land: Law of Property Act 1925, s.1(1), the other being the fee simple absolute in possession.

To develop the concept further, "real property" (a historic term derived from the Latin "res" meaning "thing") concerns immovable things such as land and those things attached to land like buildings. It is distinct from "personal property" meaning, broadly, anything which is not real property; moveable things such as a car (tangible) or stocks and shares (intangible). There is yet a further distinction within the category of personal property: chattels real and chattels personal. One might think that a tenancy – being an estate in land – would be "real property" but that is not so. Largely as a result of its time-limited nature, leases historically were categorised as "personal property" and became the main component of the sub-category "chattels real" (alongside other specific interests in land). Any personal property which is not a lease or other specified interest in land is therefore part of the "chattels personal" sub-category.

Why do we need to know this? Because it helps with understanding the terminology used in the Administration of Estates Act 1925 ("AEA

1925") – the source of law governing what happens to tenancies on death (amongst other things). They do not end because they become part of the deceased's "estate" on death.

So many estates, so many different contexts…

Administration of Estates Act 1925

On the death of a tenant, his "real estate" devolves on his personal representatives: s.1(1), AEA 1925. The Act defines real estate as including chattels real (i.e., leaseholds): s.3, AEA 1925.

Pausing there, the tenant's tenancy (being a chattel real and therefore part of his real estate) devolves on his personal representatives: what does it mean for his real estate to *devolve*, and who are his *personal representatives*?

There is no definition of "devolve" in the AEA 1925. The Oxford Dictionary of Law defines it as "[t]he passing of property from one owner to another, which may occur on death or sale, as a gift by operation of law or in any other way" and the phrase is used interchangeably with "vests" (meaning *inter alia* "to confer legal ownership of land on someone") in many of the leading textbooks. In essence, it means the tenancy passes to the personal representative to deal with as a representative of the deceased.

In the Act, unless the context otherwise requires, "personal representative" means: "the executor, original or by representation, or administrator for the time being of a deceased person […]": s.55(1)(xi), AEA 1925.

So, does this happen automatically on the death of the tenant? It depends. If the tenant made a will and there is an executor with the power to obtain probate, the tenancy will vest in the executor under that will automatically on death: *Collis v Flower* [1921] 1 K.B. 409; *Abbey v Barnstyn* [1930] 1 K.B. 660. This is because probate merely proves the will – it does not confer executorship which is derived from the will itself. However, if the tenant died without making a will (referred to as "intestate") then no, it cannot vest in the administrator automatically, because to become an administrator, a person must apply to the court for appointment as such ("taking out letters of administration"): see *Whitehead v Palmer* [1908] 1 K.B. 151. There are no other formalities required: death of a testator tenant + executor = tenancy vests in the executor; death of an intestate tenant + letters of administration taken out by an administrator = tenancy vests in the administrator.

One point to note here (which will become relevant later in the context of ending assured tenancies where there is no succession) is that when letters of administration are granted, the law treats the title of the administrator as having arisen at the time of death: *In the Goods of Pryse* [1902] P. 301; *Youngmin v Heath* [1974] 1 W.L.R. 135. This is known as the doctrine of "relation back".

Youngmin v Heath concerned a claim, not for possession of property but rather rent payable in respect of a tenancy of that property where the tenant had died intestate. Mr Heath had taken out letters of administration. On the landlord's claim for rent arrears, Lord Denning held the following:

a) On the death intestate of the tenant, the tenancy did not determine and instead vested in what was then the Probate judge but is now the Public Trustee: see s.9, AEA 1925.

b) When letters of administration were granted, the administrator became entitled to the tenancy in that capacity and his title related back to the time when the tenant died: see *In The Goods of Pryse* [1904] P. 301. The effect of this was that the administrator was – as administrator – entitled to the tenancy from the very moment the tenant died.

c) It is an implied term of a tenancy that the obligation to pay rent continues *during the currency of the tenancy* which binds the tenant

> and his personal representative to pay rent so long as the tenancy continues — that is until it is determined by proper notice to terminate it. The personal representative must fulfil the obligation to pay the rent, but only to the extent of the assets in his hands: see *Williams on Executors and Administrators.* 14th ed. (1960), vol. 2, p. 1032; and *Megarry and Wade, The Law of Real Property*, 3rd ed. (1966). p. 733.

Therefore, in this case, the administrator was liable for the rent (to the extent of the deceased's assets) until the tenancy was properly determined by notice to quit. This doctrine was relied on in Fred Long & Sons v Burgess [1950] 1 K.B. 115 to argue unsuccessfully that where a tenancy had vested in the administrator, a notice to quit was ineffective to end a tenancy. The Court held that relation-back did not defeat a prior validly served notice to quit.

But what happens to the tenancy where a tenant dies intestate and an administrator has yet to be appointed, or where there is a will but no executor with the power to obtain probate?

Enter the Public Trustee…

The role of the Public Trustee

By s.9(1) and (2), AEA 1925,[1]

> "(1) Where a person dies intestate, his real and personal estate shall vest in the Public Trustee until the grant of administration.
>
> (2) Where a testator dies and—

---

[1] Substituted by Law of Property (Miscellaneous Provisions) Act 1994, s.14(1) from July 1, 1995.

> (a) at the time of his death there is no executor with the power to obtain probate of the will, or
>
> (b) at any time before probate of the will is granted there ceases to be any executor with power to obtain probate,
>
> the real and personal estate of which he disposes by the will shall vest in the Public Trustee until the grant of representation."

"The vesting of real or personal estate in the Public Trustee by virtue of this section does not confer on him any beneficial interest in, or impose on him any duty, obligation or liability in respect of, the property": s.9(3), AEA 1925. The Public Trustee therefore essentially acts as a "repository of title"; a shelf on which the tenancy sits awaiting its vesting in the administrator or, less commonly, a newly appointed executor. Some older cases refer to title vesting in the "President of the Family Division" which was the previous such "repository of title" in similar circumstances prior to 1995.

Who might be a successor?

In many cases, the relevant provisions of the statutory schemes in England governing both fixed-term and periodic secure tenancies, and assured tenancies which are periodic or for a fixed term of not less than two years and which contain an express term for succession, will determine who is entitled to succeed (whether directly or by giving effect to express terms in the tenancy agreement). In Wales, the statutory scheme insofar as it applies to social rented occupation contracts only concerns periodic contracts. This is dealt with in detail in the relevant chapters.

In England, fixed-term secure tenancies (including flexible tenancies) devolve in the manner described above under the tenant's will or under the intestacy rules: s.90, Housing Act 1985. However, if they devolve on a person not entitled to succeed under s.89, they cease to be secure and (if granted after 2012) they can be ended by service of a notice. If granted before 1.4.12, it may be much harder to recover possession from a non-qualified successor if there is no break clause or other means of bringing the tenancy to an end. The lease terms will govern and should be checked through with a fine-tooth comb.

Categories of successor

In broad terms, for periodic tenancies, the English statutes treat survivorship (where one joint tenant dies) as succession and, after 31.3.12, only permit succession otherwise to spouses or civil partners residing with the tenant when s/he dies, or to family members (including those living with the tenant as if they were married or in a civil partnership), in the absence of such a spouse etc. if the tenancy agreement expressly provides for such a succession: s.86A, Housing Act 1985 (inserted by Localism Act 2011). If the tenancy was granted before 1.4.12, prescribed family members qualify to succeed if they resided with the tenant when s/he dies and also resided with them for the period of a year immediately before their death: s.87, Housing Act 1985.

Since 1.12.22, in Wales, similar categories of persons qualify as successors, with spouses etc. taking priority and other family members being in reserve. Qualifying carers now form a category of successor too: RH(W) Act 2016, ss.73-83 and 139.

But what if a tenant e.g., wills his tenancy to his resident daughter who lived with him for six months immediately before his death, but the resident son lived there for more than 12 months before death? This is dealt with by the main statutory schemes in the following way. Where a person is entitled to succeed under the statute the tenancy vests in that successor automatically and there is no vesting under the will or on intestacy: see s.17(1), Housing Act 1988 as an example (dealt with in Chapter 4).

It is important to appreciate that in the context of most social housing tenancies, the statute itself dictates the qualifying successor but there may e.g., be more than one which qualifies (see the relevant chapters on secure, assured and other tenancies and succession in Wales) to succeed under the tenancy or the contract may provide for selection. In such cases, if a person is named in the former tenant's will or would be entitled under the intestacy rules (see s.46, AEA 1925) this may affect the selection if, in default of agreement, it is left to the local authority (in the case of secure tenancies) or the court (in the case of assured tenancies) to select the person who succeeds.

How does the successor get the tenancy?

A successor now obtains the tenancy by operation of the applicable statutory scheme where relevant.

Where a statutory scheme does not apply, it is established authority that neither a legatee or devisee of leaseholds (meaning the person entitled under the will to the tenancy) nor a person entitled to a tenancy under the intestacy rules becomes the tenant at law or in equity[2] until the executor(s) or administrator(s) have assented to the bequest: see *Clarion Housing Association v Carter* [2021] EWHC 2890 (QB); [2022] H.L.R. 10 considered later in Chapter 4.

The assent must be in writing, signed by all the personal representatives who have proved: see Administration of Estates Act 1925 ss.36(4), 2(2).

[2] An equitable tenant is one who does not hold the legal title to the tenancy for example because the formalities for granting the tenancy have not been fulfilled or the person is a child.

What if there is no successor?

This will be explored in more detail in the chapter on possession proceedings, but it will suffice for present purposes to set out the basic position.

In the case of a will/executor, it is likely that any tenancy of little value will simply be ended by the executor serving notice to quit on the landlord. If this is not done, then the landlord must take steps to end the tenancy.

If the tenancy is a fixed-term tenancy, the landlord may have to activate any break clause or rely on the death of the tenant as a basis for re-entry. Service of a notice to quit will be of no assistance because they apply to periodic tenancies.

It is the case with periodic tenancies that they continue after the tenant's death: *Parker d. Walker v Constable* (1769) 3 Wils. 25. Resultantly, the landlord must determine the tenancy by notice to quit before seeking possession: *Wirral BC v Smith* (1981–82) 4 H.L.R. 81 CA. Thus, the one thing the Public Trustee can do during this period is receive a copy of a notice to quit (necessarily from the landlord) to end the tenancy vested in him: *Epping Forest D.C. v Pomphrett* [1990] 2 E.G.L.R. 46.

For assured tenancies, where a notice to quit is not served and the tenancy is assented to a person in occupation of the property as his or her only or principal home but who is not entitled to succeed, the landlord can rely on Ground 7, Housing Act 1988.

Points to note:

- Tenancies do not end on the death of the tenant. They continue until terminated in accordance with their terms.
- A tenancy forms part of a deceased person's "real estate" and devolves in accordance with either his or her will or under the rules of intestacy.
- If a tenant dies testate (with a will), the property devolves on his executors if they exist.
- If there are no executors or the tenant dies intestate, the tenancy devolves on the Public Trustee until an administrator is appointed at which point it vests in him or her.
- The position in Wales is now dealt with compositely with little to no scope for the application of common law or statutory rules on inheritance.

CHAPTER THREE

SECURE TENANCIES

The law on succession to secure tenancies is different in England and Wales and changed significantly from 1 April 2012 in England with the commencement of the Localism Act 2012 and recently by RH(W) Act 2016. The former Act was designed to give local authorities increased autonomy in their local decision-making. One facet of this autonomy was the ability to decide based on local priorities who (other than spouses, civil partners or those living as such) should be entitled to succeed to secure tenancies.

This Chapter considers the position in England both before and after 1 April 2012. The position in Wales is considered in Chapter 6. It examines who is qualified to succeed to a secure tenancy and how that succession occurs. It also considers what happens in the event of succession to the former tenant's right to buy.

The primary source of law is Part IV of the Housing Act 1985 (as amended).

Succession pre-Localism

Qualifying to succeed – s.87, Housing Act 1985

Where a tenancy was granted prior to 1 April 2012, by s.87, Housing Act 1985, a person is qualified to succeed a tenant (of either a periodic or fixed-term secure tenancy of a property in England) in the following circumstances:

a) The tenant was not a successor (see below); *and*

b) The person occupies the dwelling-house as his only or principal home at the time of the tenant's death; *and*

c) The person is

    i. the tenant's spouse, or

    ii. the tenant's civil partner, or

    iii. another member of the tenant's family and resided with the tenant throughout the period of twelve months ending with the tenant's death.

Separately but relatedly, where a tenancy is a joint tenancy (i.e. at least two and up to four tenants are each tenants of the whole property jointly), and one tenant dies, it vests in the remaining tenant(s) under the right of "survivorship" and the statutory succession provisions do not apply: *Solihull MBC v Hickin* [2012] UKSC 39; [2012] 1 W.L.R. 2295. As seen below, this does count as a succession for certain purposes.

Tenant not a successor – s.88, Housing Act 1985

As seen above, if the tenant is him or herself a successor, that presents a bar to any further succession. A tenant is a successor if:

a) the tenancy vested in him by virtue of s.89, Housing Act 1985 (succession to a periodic tenancy), or

b) he was a joint tenant and has become the sole tenant (normally by survivorship – i.e., where the tenant dies albeit, in theory, this could occur by a process known as "release"), or

c) the tenancy arose by virtue of s.86 (periodic tenancy arising on the ending of a fixed-term tenancy) and the first tenancy there mentioned was granted to another person or jointly to him and another person, or

d) he became the tenant on the tenancy being assigned to him (but subject to the exceptions in s.88(2)-(3)), or

e) he became the tenant on the tenancy being vested in him on the death of the previous tenant, or

f) the tenancy was previously an introductory tenancy, and he was a successor to the introductory tenancy: s.88(1).

The exceptions to a deemed succession by virtue of an assignment are in s.88(2)-(3) and comprise the following:

a) where a tenancy is assigned pursuant to an order under s.24, Matrimonial Causes Act 1973 or s.17(1) of the Matrimonial and Family Proceedings Act 1984 the assignee tenant is a successor only if the other party to the marriage was a successor. Thus, the assignor spouse's succession rights transfer to the assignee spouse unaffected by the assignment.

b) The position outlined above also applies to assignment from one civil partner to the other under Part 2 of Schedule 5, or paragraph 9(2) or (3) of Schedule 7, to the Civil Partnership Act 2004 (property adjustment orders in connection with civil partnership proceedings or after the overseas dissolution of civil partnership, etc.).

c) Where a tenant assigns his tenancy pursuant to a mutual exchange under s.92, Housing Act 1985, any succession rights he had in relation to the tenancy he exchanged go with him to the property of which he is now the tenant. The mutual exchange does not affect his succession rights.

Finally, in relation to s.88, we have subsection (4) which provides that where within six months of the coming to an end of a secure tenancy which is a periodic tenancy ("the former tenancy") the tenant becomes a tenant under another secure tenancy which is a periodic tenancy, and

(a) the tenant was a successor in relation to the former tenancy, and

(b) under the other tenancy either the dwelling-house or the landlord, or both, are the same as under the former tenancy,

the tenant is also a successor in relation to the other tenancy unless the agreement creating that tenancy otherwise provides.

Strictly speaking, s.88(4) does not bar succession as a result of a previous succession; what it does is ensure (subject to the inclusion of an express term to the contrary in any new agreement) that where a person succeeds to a periodic secure tenancy, he or she retains that successor status if – within six months – they are granted a new periodic secure tenancy either of the same property with or without the same landlord, or of an alternative property but with the same landlord of other accommodation. This would mean that if possession of the property was obtained on the grounds of under-occupation, any new tenancy of smaller accommodation would remain subject to the prior succession despite a new tenancy agreement being granted so long as either the property or the landlord remained the same.

Only or principal home

The person wanting to succeed must have occupied the property as their only or principal home at the time of the former tenant's death.

The concept of "only or principal home" is one found in s.81, Housing Act 1985 and s.1(1)(b), Housing Act 1988 and amongst other things confers the status of secure or assured on an otherwise contractual tenancy. The use of the phrase in the context of succession serves to ensure that there is a sufficient nexus between the person who would succeed and his/her occupation of the property subject to the tenancy. Accordingly, for a tenancy to attract security of tenure under the Housing Act 1985 and Housing Act 1988 (i.e. secure or assured status), the tenant must occupy the demised property as his/her only or principal home.

The only or principal home element of the tenant condition is ambulatory in its effect i.e., a tenant can go in and out of assured status: *Basingstoke & Deane BC v Paice* (1995) 27 H.L.R. 433, CA and *Manchester CC v Finn* [2003] H.L.R. 41, CA at 32.

In deciding which of two homes an applicant occupies as his only or principal home, where a tenant sleeps is a factor of the utmost importance: *Sumeghova v McMahon* [2002] EWCA Civ 1581; [2003] H.L.R. 26.

Whether a person occupies premises as their only or principal home is a question of fact and degree: *Crawley BC v Sawyer* (1988) 20 HLR 98, CA. In *Crawley*, T left his secure tenancy to live with his girlfriend. The gas and electricity to his home were subsequently cut off, and the following year he informed the local authority, L, that he was living with his girlfriend and that they intended to purchase her home. L instituted possession proceedings. By the time of the hearing T had split up with his girlfriend and was again living in the premises. He gave evidence that he had not abandoned the premises and had every intention of returning to them. The judge found that T continued to pay rent and rates while he was absent, visited the premises once a month and at some time spent a week at the premises. He held that the premises were at all times T's principal home.

On appeal, the Court of Appeal considered the terminology of the nearest Rent Act 1977 equivalent "if and so long as he occupies the dwelling-house as his residence" and concluded that there was no material difference between occupying premises as a home and occupying them as a residence. It is not necessary to show actual physical occupation of the home. Whether a home is occupied as the tenant's principal home is a *matter of fact* for the court at first instance: the judge had been entitled to take the view that the property was T's principal home throughout.

Test

In *Islington LBC v Boyle and Collier* [2011] EWCA Civ 1450, the Court of Appeal summarised the relevant principles to be applied in determining whether a tenant occupies a dwelling as his only or principal home, despite currently living elsewhere. The tenant was absent from the council property for a lengthy period, having gone to live with her father (to provide care). That this was the case was *accepted* by the tenant.

Lord Justice Etherton (at [55]) considered the proper approach where a person had ceased to occupy a property as his *only* home and held that it was a question of fact and degree in each case, but *a sufficiently lengthy or continuous absence from the dwelling could compel the inference* that the tenant had ceased to occupy the property as his only or principal home; *if that inference arose*, then the onus was on the tenant to rebut it; in order to do so, the tenant must establish that he had an intention to return and that there was a "practical" or "real" possibility of that occurring within a reasonable time; and there also needed to be some "formal, outward and visible" sign of the intention to return. Such matters had to be considered carefully.

He went on (at [64]-[65]) to consider the position where a tenant was physically present at two homes, and one had to determine which was the principal home.

> "64 In carrying out that assessment of the defendant's intention and belief, and the objective reality of the situation, there is an obvious distinction between, on the one hand, the case where the defendant has voluntarily taken up long term residence in one of two or more homes which the defendant owns or has some other enforceable right to occupy, and, on the other hand, other situations. Even in the former case, of course, the position will depend on all the facts.
>
> 65 In the light of the cases, I would summarise as follows the principles (in some cases reflecting those in [55] above) which apply to the identification of which of two or more homes of the tenant is or was the tenant's principal home. First, the

> length or other circumstances of the tenant's absence may raise the inference that the dwelling which is the subject of the proceedings ceased to be the tenant's principal home so as to cast on the tenant the burden of proving the contrary. Secondly, in order to rebut that presumption, it is not sufficient for the tenant to prove that at the material time it was his or her subjective intention and belief that the dwelling remained the principal home. The objective facts must bear out the reality of that belief and intention both in the sense that the intention and belief are or were genuinely held and also that the intention and belief themselves reflect reality. The reason for the absence, the length and other circumstances of the absence and (where relevant) the anticipated future duration of the absence, as well as statements and conduct of the tenant, will all be relevant to that objective assessment. Thirdly, the court's focus is on the enduring intention of the tenant, which, depending on the circumstances, may not be displaced by fleeting changes of mind. Fourthly, the issue is one of fact to be determined in the light of the evidence as a whole, and in respect of which the trial judge's findings of primary fact can only be overturned on appeal if they were perverse in the sense that I have mentioned earlier; but the appeal court may in an appropriate case substitute its own inferences drawn from those primary facts."

Finally, in *Havering LBC v Dove* [2017] EWCA Civ 156, Lewison LJ reinforced the correctness of this approach when he said (at [22]):

> "In my judgment these principles [at paragraph 65 of *Boyle*] are engaged not only where the tenant is absent from the property in the sense of not being physically present at all. They are also engaged where the tenant ceases to occupy the property as his or her only or main home even if he or she continues to occupy it as a home; as, for example, where what had once been the tenant's only home becomes no more than a weekend or holiday home. Moreover, the question of an intention to return

(which often features in these cases) is in reality an intention to revert to a previous pattern of existence."

So, what can we take from the above? At the time the tenant dies, the potential successor must occupy the property as his/her only or principal home. That does not mean they must have been physically present at the property at the time of death, nor does it mean they cannot have been temporarily absent e.g., on holiday. It requires the landlord in the first instance and the court in the event of a dispute to assess the quality of the potential successor's occupation and decide whether the objective evidence supports a subjective and enduring belief on the potential successor's part that the property was their only or principal home.

Evidence

The type of evidence that one might expect to see to support such a subjective and enduring belief includes:

- Debit and credit card usage in the area surrounding the property;
- Deliveries being made to the property in the potential successor's name;
- GP registration;
- School registration;
- Next of kin and residential address listed at work or for benefits purposes;
- Address listed at HMRC if relevant;
- DVLA and vehicle insurance registration;

- Evidence from neighbours stating that the person is seen at the property;
- A cogent explanation for any lengthy absence from the property e.g. moved for temporary work purposes or a gap year etc.

Spouse/civil partner

Ordinarily, it will be straightforward to establish whether a couple are married as they will have a marriage certificate (or will be able to obtain one with relative ease from the General or Local Register Office). In circumstances where a marriage was not registered in the UK, the spouses may have a certificate granted by the country in which they were married or, failing that, may have completed a sworn affidavit attesting to the marriage.

Since 13 March 2014, same-sex couples have been able to marry in the same way as opposite-sex couples: Marriage (Same Sex Couples) Act 2013.

The Civil Partnership Act 2004 s.1 identifies the elements of a civil partnership as two people who are of the same sex and register their relationship in the prescribed way. The amendments made by Civil Partnership Act 2004 Sch.8 ensure that civil partners enjoy the same status in respect of housing rights as married couples. The civil partnership confers rights and responsibilities on the parties to it that are akin to the rights and responsibilities of a married couple. The partnership is evidenced by a certificate similar to that evidencing a marriage.

Another member of the tenant's family

If the person is not the tenant's spouse or civil partner, they will nonetheless be qualified to succeed to the tenancy if they are another member of the tenant's family and resided with the tenant throughout the period of twelve months ending with the tenant's death.

Section 113, Housing Act 1985 provides a definition of members of a person's family.

> "(1) A person is a member of another's family within the meaning of this Part if—
>
> (a) he is the spouse or civil partner of that person, or he and that person live together as husband and wife or as if they were civil partners, or
>
> (b) he is that person's parent, grandparent, child, grandchild, brother, sister, uncle, aunt, nephew or niece.
>
> (2) For the purpose of subsection (1)(b)—
>
> (a) a relationship by marriage or civil partnership shall be treated as a relationship by blood,
>
> (b) a relationship of the half-blood shall be treated as a relationship of the whole blood,
>
> (c) the stepchild of a person shall be treated as his child, and
>
> (d) an illegitimate child shall be treated as the legitimate child of his mother and reputed father."

It should be noted that the definition includes spouses and civil partners, but they are excluded from consideration in context because they are catered for separately under s.87. We are concerned with *another* member of the tenant's family which includes persons living together as a spouse or civil partner. Advisors should take care to ensure that such persons are not equiparated with spouses and civil partners as they must satisfy the 12-month residency requirement and their priority for succession is different (which we will look at later). In *Turley v (1) Wandsworth LBC (2) Secretary of State for Communities and Local Government* [2017] EWCA Civ 189, the Court of Appeal held that the 12-month residence requirement to unmarried couples is compatible with Arts 8 and 14, European Convention on Human Rights 1950 as it pursues the legitimate aim of seeking to provide a reliable basis for assessing whether two people are living together in a sufficiently permanent and lasting relationship so as to be treated as if they were spouses.

Insofar as it governs statutory succession, this definition is exhaustive. In *Sheffield CC v Wall* [2010] EWCA Civ 922 the Court of Appeal held that a foster child was not a child for the purposes of s.113 and therefore did not qualify to succeed to her foster mother/father's tenancy.

The fact it limits rights of succession to those listed has been held not to breach Arts 8 and 14, European Convention on Human Rights 1950: *Wandsworth LBC v Michalak* [2002] EWCA Civ 271; [2002] 4 All ER 1136. The rationale is that any discrimination is justified on the basis of the need to allocate social housing which involves a deliberate policy choice by Parliament.

Cohabitants

As we've already seen, cohabitants may be "another member of the tenant's family" under s.87 if they can demonstrate that they live together as spouses or civil partners.

So, what quality of cohabitation is sufficient to demonstrate that the parties are living together as spouses or civil partners?

a) Whether or not persons are living together as spouses or civil partners is in part a question of intention: in *City of Westminster v Peart* (1992) 24 H.L.R. 389, CA, a couple who had reconciled were held not to be living together as husband and wife, on the facts of the case including particularly that the defendant had another flat. See by way of further example, *Amicus Horizon Ltd v (1) The Estate of Judy Mabott (deceased) (2) Antony Brand* [2012] EWCA Civ 895; [2012] H.L.R. 42.

b) Sexual relations are relevant but not determinative: by way of example, where a couple shared occupation of a two-room flat but slept in separate rooms and had not spoken for several months the Court of Appeal nonetheless found they were living together as husband and wife (a rather sorry testament to the institution!): *Adeoso v Adeoso* [1980] 1 W.L.R. 1535, CA.

c) Casual and intermittent relations could not qualify as family but a stable relationship could do so: *Dyson Holdings v Fox* [1976] Q.B. 503. The longer the relationship, the easier it is to infer a family relationship: *Chios Property Investment Co. Ltd. v Lopez* [1988] 1 E.G.L.R. 98.

d) Same-sex relationships of sufficient quality to amount to living together as civil partners are now included. This was a hard-fought issue as shown by the cases of *Ghaidan-Mendoza* [2004] 2 A.C. 557, applied in *Nutting v Southern Housing Group* [2004] EWHC 2982 (Ch) and subsequently by the amendments introduced by the Civil Partnership Act 2004.

<u>Adoption</u>

A legally adopted child is treated as if a natural child: Children Act 2004 s.8 and Sch.1.

Twelve months' residency

Prior to the Localism Act 2012, under the Housing Act 1985 and subject to satisfaction of the matters referred to herein, members of the deceased tenant's family (see above) are entitled to succeed if they resided with the tenant for the period of 12 months. This is a question of fact.

So, what quality of living together is needed to establish "residency with"?

There is a plethora of decisions which deal with this issue. The key factors are set out below.

a) The word "with" is important and means more than residing at the same premises as the deceased: see e.g., *R (CN) v Lewisham LBC; R (ZH) v Newham LBC* [2014] UKSC 62; [2015] A.C. 1259.

b) The burden of proof is on the potential successor to show residence with the deceased.

c) The concept of residing does not require immediate presence; accordingly, if a person goes into hospital and dies there or moves in with a family member to receive care after an accident for a period of time it will not automatically prevent a succession from taking place: *Tompkins v Rowley* [1949] E.G.D. 314, CA; *Hedgedale Ltd v Hards* (1990) 23 T.L.R. 158, CA.

d) A temporary absence from the property by the potential successor likewise does not automatically defeat succession: going on holiday, visiting family or even moving out with a view to living with someone else which is not guaranteed can nonetheless amount to continued residency so long as there is an "intention to return" i.e. a continuing connection with the premises despite physical absence: *Camden LBC v Goldenberg* (1996) 28 H.L.R. 727, CA.

e) Conversely, physical presence at the property on a regular basis (including sleeping there overnight 3-4 times a week) may be insufficient to amount to residency if the quality of presence at the property does not constitute a settled home and becoming part of the deceased's household: *Swanbrae Ltd v Elliott* (1986) 19 H.L.R. 86, CA (where a daughter caring for her sick mother retained her own flat). This should be contrasted with *Hildebrand v Moon* (1989) 22 H.L.R. 1, CA, where a daughter caring for her mother also retained her own flat but where the evidence showed that she had moved in with her mum "permanently".

f) In *Islington LBC v Freeman* [2009] EWCA Civ 536; [2009] 24 E.G. 85 (CS), the Court of Appeal reviewed the authorities on the meaning of "residing with" and held that it means more than physical presence or even satisfaction of the only or principal home test; it involved looking at the claimant's actions and ascertaining whether they exhibited a "home-making intention" rather than merely staying with the tenant for a limited time and a limited purpose: *per* Jacob LJ at [28] and [33].

g) The phrase "resided with" does not mean residency only at the subject property. It will be sufficient for a potential successor to show residency (pursuant to any tenure) with the deceased at other premises: *Waltham Forest LBC v Thomas* (1992) 24 H.L.R. 622, HL. Accordingly, prior residence before an approach as homeless or mutual exchange will be enough.

How succession occurs

<u>Periodic tenancies – s.89, Housing Act 1985</u>

This section is concerned with "periodic" tenancies i.e., tenancies which run from week to week or month to month or year to year. This is to be contrasted with a "fixed-term" tenancy which is a defined period of time e.g., "for a term of 2 years beginning on X date".

Section 89 applies where a secure tenant dies and the tenancy is periodic: s.89(1).

Where there is a person qualified to succeed the tenant, the tenancy vests by virtue of s.89 in that person, or if there is more than one such person in the one to be preferred in accordance with the following rules:

a) the tenant's spouse or civil partner is to be preferred to another member of the tenant's family; and

b) of two or more other members of the tenant's family such of them is to be preferred as may be agreed between them or as may, where there is no such agreement, be selected by the landlord: s.89(2).

By s.89(3), where there is no person qualified to succeed the tenant, the tenancy ceases to be a secure tenancy in the following circumstances:

a) when it is vested or otherwise disposed of in the course of the administration of the tenant's estate, save where the vesting or other disposal is the result of an order of the court made under

    i. s.24 of the Matrimonial Causes Act 1973 (property adjustment orders made in connection with matrimonial proceedings),

    ii. s.17(1) of the Matrimonial and Family Proceedings Act 1984 (property adjustment orders after overseas divorce, &c.),

    iii. paragraph 1 of Schedule 1 to the Children Act 1989 (orders for financial relief against parents),

    iv. Part 2 of Schedule 5, or paragraph 9(2) or (3) of Schedule 7, to the Civil Partnership Act 2004 (property adjustment orders in connection with civil partnership proceedings or after overseas dissolution of civil partnership, etc.); or

b) when it is known that when the tenancy is so vested or disposed of it will not be in pursuance of such an order.

Broadly speaking, the aforementioned statutory provisions at s.89(3) govern what happens to property (including tenancies) on the separation of couples whether with or without children. A local authority will need to request copies of any such order made in the Family Court from the potential successor.

A tenancy which ceases to be a secure tenancy by virtue of s.89 cannot subsequently become a secure tenancy: s.89(4). Section 89(4) is critical to the question of ending the tenancy by notice to quit which is considered in Chapter 8. Unlike the occupation of a property as one's only or principal home pursuant to the tenant condition in s.79, Housing Act 1985, where one can go in and out of secure status as a tenant depending on whether you are occupying the property as a home or not (sometimes referred to in the authorities and academic texts as "ambulatory effect"), where secure status is lost under s.89 owing to a failed succession, it cannot be regained.

Fixed term tenancies – s.90, Housing Act 1985

Having catered for periodic tenancies in s.89, s.90 covers secure fixed-term tenancies ("term certain" meaning "fixed-term") (this is especially relevant to the flexible tenancies insofar as they have been adopted in the wake of the Localism Act 2012).

Section 90 applies where a secure tenant dies, and the tenancy is for a "term certain": s.90(1).

By s.90(2), the tenancy remains a secure tenancy until:

a) it is vested or otherwise disposed of in the course of the administration of the tenant's estate at which point it ceases to be secure unless

a. the vesting or other disposal is in pursuance of an order made under the same statutory provisions referred to above in respect of s.89(3);

b. the vesting or other disposal is to a person qualified to succeed the tenant; or

b) it is known that when it is so vested or disposed of it will not be a secure tenancy: s.90(2) and (3).

Mirroring the position for periodic tenancies, a fixed-term tenancy which ceases to be a secure tenancy by virtue of s.90 cannot subsequently become a secure tenancy: s.90(4).

Succession post-Localism

The Localism Act 2012, s.160 inserted a new s.86A into the Housing Act 1985. It only applies to tenancies of properties in England and only when that tenancy was granted after 1 April 2012: Localism Act 2011 (Commencement No.4 and Transitional, Transitory and Saving Provisions) Order 2012 (SI 2012/628) art.6(a) subject to transitional provisions in arts 9, 11, 14, 15 and 17.

Section 86A provides:

> "**86A Persons qualified to succeed tenant: England**
>
> (1) A person ("P") is qualified to succeed the tenant under a secure tenancy of a dwelling-house in England if—
>
> (a) P occupies the dwelling-house as P's only or principal home at the time of the tenant's death, and
>
> (b) P is the tenant's spouse or civil partner.

(2) A person ("P") is qualified to succeed the tenant under a secure tenancy of a dwelling-house in England if—

  (a) at the time of the tenant's death the dwelling-house is not occupied by a spouse or civil partner of the tenant as his or her only or principal home,

  (b) an express term of the tenancy makes provision for a person other than such a spouse or civil partner of the tenant to succeed to the tenancy, and

  (c) P's succession is in accordance with that term.

(3) Subsection (1) or (2) does not apply if the tenant was a successor as defined in section 88.

(4) In such a case, a person ("P") is qualified to succeed the tenant if—

  (a) an express term of the tenancy makes provision for a person to succeed a successor to the tenancy, and

  (b) P's succession is in accordance with that term.

(5) For the purposes of this section, a person who was living with the tenant as if they were a married couple or civil partners is to be treated as the tenant's spouse or civil partner.

(6) Subsection (7) applies if, on the death of the tenant, there is by virtue of subsection (5) more than one person who fulfils the condition in subsection (1)(b).

(7) Such one of those persons as may be agreed between them or as may, where there is no such agreement, be

selected by the landlord is for the purpose of this section to be treated as the tenant's spouse or civil partner."

It can be seen from close consideration of the section that for tenancies granted after 1 April 2012, generally succession rights are now limited to spouses, civil partners and those who were living with the tenant as if they were spouses or civil partners at the time of death.

All is not necessarily lost for family members of a secure tenant because landlords can (if they so desire) include express provision in their tenancy agreements qualifying others (not limited to family members under s.113 but including e.g. carers or more distant relatives) to succeed on the tenant's death: s.86A(2). It is therefore critical for legal advisors and those acting in person to obtain and carefully consider any written tenancy agreement granted after 1 April 2012 to see if there are any express terms governing succession rights.

A new and welcome change to the statutory scheme is that the giving effect to an express term governing succession no longer requires the grant of a new tenancy: the tenancy now vests automatically in the successor by operation of statute: s.89(1A).

What happens to the rights enjoyed by tenants under a secure tenancy on succession?

The big one is the right to buy. This is a right enjoyed by secure tenants – in broad terms – to purchase their home at a discount if they have lived there or elsewhere as a public sector tenant for a minimum period (currently two or three years depending on when the tenancy came into being – s.119 Housing Act 1985 as amended by s.180 Housing Act 2004 and s.28 Deregulation Act 2015). The longer a tenant has lived at the property, the bigger the discount: see Part V, Housing Act 1985.

The position for spouses is that the time the deceased tenant occupied the property as a sole or joint tenant counts towards the successor's qualifying period. This also applies where a former spouse of the deceased was the tenant and the deceased lived with them as their only or principal home: Schedule 4, paragraph 2, Housing Act 1985.

When a person succeeds to their parent's tenancy, the time the deceased tenant occupied the property is added to the time the successor builds up: Schedule 4, paragraph 4, Housing Act 1985. In essence, the successor "steps into the shoes" of the former tenant for the purpose of the qualifying period for the right to buy.

Points of note:

- The position on succession differs according to whether the tenancy is in England or Wales and, in England, whether the tenancy was granted before or after 1 April 2012.

- Succession rights for secure tenants prior to 1 April 2012 were more extensive and included alongside spouses, civil partners and those living together as such, succession by family members as of right. Now such familial successions must appear expressly in the terms and conditions of tenancy.

- The same changes which restricted familial successions under statute have expanded the right to other persons at the discretion of the local authority.

- The residency criteria for succession are complex and should be considered carefully on the facts.

- Joint tenants do not succeed on the death of one under statute or at common law. They inherit the tenancy under the principle of "survivorship". This is deemed a succession for the purposes of the one succession rule.

CHAPTER FOUR

ASSURED TENANCIES

In England, assured tenancies are increasingly forming the bedrock of social housing in modern times. Local authorities increasingly discharge their housing functions through the allocation of tenancies of private registered providers of social housing or through private landlords. Neither can grant secure tenancies (albeit the former can "inherit" secure tenancies via stock transfers in limited circumstances).

The governing legislation is the Housing Act 1988 and particularly s.17 thereof.

There are specific definitions of certain terms used below. It is important for advisors to establish whether the tenancy is indeed assured. The mere fact it is a tenancy of a private registered provider is not determinative: see s.1, Housing Act 1988 which sets out that tenancies of "social landlords" in layman's terms are nonetheless assured.

Section 45 of the Housing Act 1988 defines the following material terms:

- "dwelling house" includes a house or part of a house;
- "fixed-term tenancy" means any tenancy other than a periodic tenancy;
- "landlord" includes any person from time to time deriving title under the original landlord (e.g., an intermediate landlord) and also includes, in relation to a dwelling-house, any person other than a tenant who is, or but for the existence of an assured tenancy would be, entitled to possession of the dwelling-house (which would include e.g., a trustee in bankruptcy or such like);

- "tenancy" includes a sub-tenancy and an agreement for a tenancy or sub-tenancy; and

- "tenant" includes a sub-tenant and any person deriving title under the original tenant or sub-tenant.

Similar to secure tenancies, for assured tenancies, there is strictly no such thing as succession on the death of a joint tenant. The tenancy becomes held by the remaining live tenants by operation of the doctrine of survivorship. This is "deemed" to be a succession for the purposes of the rule against two or more statutory successions (unless the landlord exercises its discretion in the express terms of the tenancy agreement to confer more). So, without more, if you survived to a joint tenancy then you are a successor under both s.89, Housing Act 1985 (as we saw in the previous chapter) and s.17, Housing Act 1988.

Again, the commencement of the Localism Act 2012 changed a number of things about how succession worked for assured tenancies granted after 1 April 2012 (it seems to the author, for the better, as it introduced a relatively composite scheme for statutory succession which did away with the need to worry about how to give effect to a contractual succession, how to grant new tenancies where a discretion to allow a "non-statutory succession" was retained and what the interplay was with common law and statutory rules governing what happened to tenancies on death (see Chapter 2).

The general principles applicable below are considered in detail in Chapter 3.

Pre-Localism Act 2012

The position prior to the introduction of the Localism Act 2012 (and still applicable to tenancies granted prior to that date) was simplistic but narrow. It simply provided for a single succession to a spouse and eventually also a civil partner and those living together as such: s.17(1) and (4).

By s.17(2), successors were those who had succeeded by dint of s.17 or under the will or intestacy of the deceased, survivors to a former joint tenancy and those who succeeded to tenancies under the Rent Act 1977 or Rent (Agriculture) Act 1976 pursuant to s.39(5), Housing Act 1988. A further category was those who succeeded to a tenancy and were granted a new tenancy of the same or substantially the same property and remained the tenant of that property throughout after succeeding: s.17(3).

Competing successors had to agree on who would succeed between themselves or the matter would have to be determined by the County Court: s.17(5).

In order for private registered providers of social housing to expand the categories of successor (particularly in circumstances where e.g., they bought local authority stock under large-scale voluntary stock transfers and the tenants went from secure with relatively expansive succession rights to assured with much less by way of security in this regard) the private providers undertook to and did include terms in their tenancy agreements which attempted to preserve those rights for the transferring tenants (and more importantly their potential successors).

Prior to the Localism Act 2012 (which you will see below placed contractual succession on a statutory footing), a contractual term – in a tenancy pre-dating the commencement of the Contract (Rights of Third Parties) Act 1999 – which permitted a family member to succeed was widely viewed as being incapable of enforcement owing to issues surrounding the rights of third parties to enforce a contract (themselves remedied in most part by the Contract (Rights of Third Parties) Act 1999). This problem was identified and decided as late as in 2021, where the High Court held that such a term could take effect as a trust of a promise which was capable of being enforced by the purported successor: *Clarion Housing Association Ltd v Carter* [2021] EWHC 2890 (QB).

Such contractual "succession" cannot take effect by way of the tenancy vesting automatically in the contractual "successor" because the tenancy must devolve under the tenant's will or the rules of intestacy. This led to new tenancies being granted in some cases and possession claims in others. It was unsatisfactory for both contractual successors and landlords.

Post-Localism Act 2012

Succession to periodic tenancy by spouse etc.

By s.17, Housing Act 1988, in England, unless there has previously been a succession (as to which see below) a spouse or civil partner (or those living together as such – s.17(4)) succeeds to an assured periodic tenancy and the tenancy automatically vests in them and does not devolve under the tenant's will or intestacy if:

a) the sole tenant under an assured periodic tenancy dies, and

b) immediately before the death, the tenant's spouse or civil partner was occupying the dwelling-house as his or her only or principal home: s.17(1).

Further, and again save where there has already been a succession, a tenancy vests in a person and does not devolve under the tenant's will or intestacy where, in any case:

a) there is an assured periodic tenancy of a dwelling house in England under which

    i. the landlord is a private registered provider of social housing, and

    ii. the tenant is the sole tenant,

b) the tenant under the tenancy dies,

c) immediately before the death, the dwelling-house was not occupied by a spouse or civil partner of the tenant as his or her only or principal home,

d) an express term of the tenancy makes provision for a person other than such a spouse or civil partner of the tenant to succeed to the tenancy, and

e) there is a person whose succession is in accordance with that term: s.17(1A).

Succession to PRP fixed-term tenancy of 2+ years by spouse etc.

Again, save where there has already been a succession, on the death of the tenant, the tenancy vests by virtue of s.17 in the spouse or civil partner (and does not devolve under the tenant's will or intestacy) in any case where:

a) there is an assured tenancy of a dwelling house in England for a fixed term of not less than two years under which

    i. the landlord is a private registered provider of social housing, and

    ii. the tenant is the sole tenant,

b) the tenant under the tenancy dies, and

c) immediately before the death, the tenant's spouse or civil partner was occupying the dwelling-house as his or her only or principal home: s.17(1B).

Succession to PRP fixed-term tenancy of 2+ years by a family member

Again, save where there has already been a succession, on the death of the tenant, the tenancy vests by virtue of s.17 in a person (and does not devolve under the tenant's will or intestacy) in any case where:

a) there is an assured tenancy of a dwelling house in England for a fixed term of not less than two years under which

    i. the landlord is a private registered provider of social housing, and

    ii. the tenant is the sole tenant,

b) the tenant under the tenancy dies,

c) immediately before the death, the dwelling-house was not occupied by a spouse or civil partner of the tenant as his or her only or principal home,

d) an express term of the tenancy makes provision for a person other than such a spouse or civil partner of the tenant to succeed to the tenancy, and

e) there is a person whose succession is in accordance with that term: s.17(1C).

Previous successor

In all the cases above if the exception that there has been a previous successor applies (see s.17(1D), then the tenancy may vest by virtue of s.17 in a person (and, accordingly, does not devolve under the tenant's will or intestacy) if, and only if:

a) in a case within s.17(1), the tenancy is of a dwellinghouse in England under which the landlord is a private registered provider of social housing,

b) an express term of the tenancy makes provision for a person to succeed a successor to the tenancy, and

c) the person's succession is in accordance with that term: s.17(1E).

Meaning of successor

By s.17(2), a tenant is a successor in relation to a tenancy if:

a) the tenancy became vested in him either by virtue of this section or under the will or intestacy of a previous tenant; or

b) at some time before the tenant's death the tenancy was a joint tenancy held by himself and one or more other persons and, prior to his death, he became the sole tenant by survivorship; or

c) he became entitled to a periodic assured tenancy on succession to what had been a Rent Act 1977 or Rent (Agriculture) Act 1976 tenancy under the former tenant (by operation of s.39(5), Housing Act 1988.

By s.17(3), a tenant remains a successor in relation to any new tenancy granted to him (alone or jointly with others) if:

a) he was a successor under an earlier tenancy of the same or substantially the same dwelling house as under the new tenancy and

b) at all times since he became such a successor he has been such a tenant of that same or substantially the same dwellinghouse.

Competing successors

Where there is more than one person in whom the tenancy could vest under s17(1A), (1C) or (1E), they must agree between themselves who will succeed in default of which (unlike secure tenancies where the landlord selects) the county court shall determine: s.17(6).

Exclusion of long leases at a premium

Section 17(7) excludes from the succession right those long leases that are assured tenancies granted on payment of a premium calculated by reference to a percentage of the value of the dwelling-house or of the cost of providing it, or under which the lessee (or the lessee's personal representatives) will or may be entitled to a sum calculated by reference, directly or indirectly, to the value of the dwelling-house. Succession to such leases remains governed by the administration of estates.

Right to acquire

There is an equivalent (albeit less available) right for certain tenants of private registered providers of social housing to buy their homes. The provisions in Part 5, Housing Act 1985 are applicable to the right to acquire: s.17(2), Housing Act 1996. Successors to assured tenancies are therefore treated analogously to their secure counterparts.

Points of note:

- Prior to the Localism Act 2012, there was a single succession right for a spouse (later also a civil partner and those living together as such). Social landlords struggled to effect contractual rights they had granted which went beyond statute.

- After the Localism Act 2012, these social landlords had free rein to have contractual succession on such express terms they saw fit and the statute provided that succession would occur automatically rather than (as had previously been the case) through the common law and legislation on the administration of estates.

- Time built up by a deceased tenant counts towards the qualifying period of his or her successor for the purposes of the right to acquire.

CHAPTER FIVE

LIMITED SECURITY OF TENURE

In a social housing context, limited security of tenure refers to those tenancies which are temporary for particular reasons. It includes assured shorthold tenancies under the Housing Act 1988 (often used as starter tenancies to assess whether a tenant will comply with their obligations pending an assured tenancy and now increasingly used to discharge local authority homelessness duties), non-secure tenancies (purely contractual tenancies) and introductory tenancies under s.124, Housing Act 1996 (like starter tenancies but of local authorities pending the grant of a secure tenancy).

Introductory tenancies

By s.131, Housing Act 1996, a person is qualified to succeed the tenant under an introductory tenancy if he occupies the dwelling-house as his only or principal home at the time of the tenant's death and either:

a) he is the tenant's spouse or civil partner, or

b) he is another member of the tenant's family and has resided with the tenant throughout the period of twelve months ending with the tenant's death,

unless, in either case, the tenant was himself a successor, as defined in s.132.

The definition of "members of a person's family" is found in s.140 and mirrors that in s.113, Housing Act 1985.

Section 132 defines who is a successor analogously to s.88, Housing Act 1985. The tenant is himself a successor if:

a) the tenancy vested in him by virtue of section 133 (succession to introductory tenancy),

b) he was a joint tenant and has become the sole tenant,

c) he became the tenant on the tenancy being assigned to him (but subject to subsections (2) and (3)), or

d) he became the tenant on the tenancy being vested in him on the death of the previous tenant.

Interestingly, a person to whom a tenancy is assigned in pursuance of an order under:

a) s.24 of the Matrimonial Causes Act 1973 (property adjustment orders in connection with matrimonial proceedings) or

b) s.17(1) of the Matrimonial and Family Proceedings Act 1984 (property adjustment orders after overseas divorce, &c) or

c) Part 2 of Schedule 5, or paragraph 9(2) or (3) of Schedule 7, to the Civil Partnership Act 2004 (property adjustment orders in connection with civil partnership proceedings or after overseas dissolution of civil partnership, etc)

is a successor only if the other party to the marriage/civil partnership was a successor: s.132(2) and (2A).

Where within six months of the coming to an end of an introductory tenancy, to which the tenant has already succeeded, the tenant becomes a tenant under another new introductory tenancy of the same dwelling house or a different dwelling house with the same landlord, the tenant is also a successor in relation to the other tenancy unless the agreement creating that tenancy otherwise provides: s.132(3).

By s.133, a person qualified to succeed is identified in the same way as for secure tenancies (i.e., by landlord selection): s.133(2), and the tenancy vests automatically in that person. If there is no person qualified to succeed, the tenancy ceases to be introductory as a secure tenancy ceased to be secure pre-Localism Act 2012: s.133(3).

As can be seen, the provision reflects closely the position in England pre-Localism Act 2012 (just to keep things interesting...). This is because the equivalent amendments which would bring introductory tenancies in line with the rules governing secure tenancies is yet to be introduced: see s.130A, Housing Act 1996 inserted by the Housing and Planning Act 2016, s.120 and Schedule 8, paragraph 7.

Non-secure tenancies

There is no statutory succession right associated with this tenure. The tenancy is contractual only and therefore can be ended on transmission under a will or on intestacy.

Assured shorthold tenancies of less than 2 years

For assured shorthold tenancies granted for a fixed term of less than two years, there is no succession right available. The position for an assured tenancy granted for 2 or more years is dealt with under Chapter 4.

Points of note

- Save in the case of an introductory tenancy where the rules for succession reflect broadly the pre-Localism Act 2012 position in England, there are no specific statutory succession rights for non-secure tenancies and assured shorthold tenancies of less than 2 years.

CHAPTER SIX

SECURE TENANCIES UNDER RENTING HOMES (WALES) ACT 2016

From 1 December 2022, succession rights in Wales are governed by RH(W) Act 2016, ss.73-83 and s.139. The provisions on succession broadly reflect the position applicable in England until 1 April 2012 and in Wales until 1 December 2022. The key differences are that references to tenants are now to sole or joint "contract-holders" and tenancies are referred to as "occupation contracts". There is also provision for two successions – a priority and a reserve. Generally, "standard contracts" apply in the private sector (and can be periodic or fixed term) and "secure contracts" apply in the "community sector" including tenancies of local authorities, registered social landlords and other types of authority (and are *periodic only*): ss.2 and 8, RH(W) Act 2016.

Secure contracts – succession under s.73

Save as catered for below, by s.73, RH(W) Act 2016, on the death of a sole contract holder under an occupation contract, if one person is qualified to succeed the contract-holder that person succeeds to the contract and if more than one person is qualified to succeed the contract-holder, the person identified in accordance with s.78 (selection from competing successors) succeeds to the contract.

Priority successor definition

By way of explanation prior to looking at the substantive provisions, a person is a "priority successor" of the contract-holder if:

a) the contract holder was not him or herself a priority successor in relation to the occupation contract (thereby barring second successions);

b) the person is the spouse or civil partner of the contract-holder, or lives together with the contract-holder as if they were spouses or civil partners, and

c) the person occupied the dwelling as his or her only or principal home at the time of the contract-holder's death: s.75

Reserve successor definition

Further, by s.76, a person is a reserve successor of the contract-holder if:

a) he or she is not a priority successor of the contract-holder and

b) he or she meets the family member condition and

c) he or she occupied the dwelling as his or her only or principal home at the time of the contract-holder's death, and

d) (if not spouse or civil partner or those living together as such – see s.250(1)(c), RH(W) Act 2016) he or she also meets the basic residence condition.

The residence condition is met if "throughout the period of 12 months ending with the contract-holder's death:

a) he or she occupied the dwelling, or

b) he or she lived with the contract-holder.

If the contract-holder was a priority successor in relation to the occupation contract, the references in subsections (2) and (3)(b) to the contract-holder include the person the contract-holder succeeded this enables a reserve successor to qualify as a second successor also: s.76(4).

So, broadly, qualification as a priority successor mirrors qualification as a spouse etc under the Housing Act 1985 and a reserve successor pursuant to s.76 broadly reflects the "other family member" qualification under the 1985 Act. Both are entitled to succeed.

Qualifying successors

Section 74, RH(W) Act 2016, identifies those qualified to succeed to an occupation contract. A person is qualified to succeed the contract-holder if that person is either a priority or a reserve successor of the contract-holder and is not excluded by dint of (i) not yet being 18 years old by the time of death or (ii) having occupied the property or part of it under a sub-occupation contract at any time within 12 months of the contract holder's death. In respect of (ii) a person is re-included as a qualifying successor if he or she is a priority successor of the contract-holder, or he or she is a reserve successor of the contract-holder who meets the family member condition in s.76(2) because of section 250(1)(a) or (b) (spouses, civil partners etc.), and the sub-occupation contract under which he or she occupied the dwelling or part of it ended before the contract-holder's death.

If the contract-holder was a reserve successor in relation to the occupation contract, no person is qualified to succeed him or her. This achieves the two-only succession rule.

Carers

An additional qualifying category for succession in Wales under RH(W) Act 2016 is carers pursuant to s.77. By this section, a person is a qualifying carer if:

a) he or she is not a priority successor of the contract-holder; and

b) he or she occupied the dwelling as his or her only or principal home at the time of the contract-holder's death; and

c) at any time in the period of 12 months ending with the contract-holder's death he or she was a carer in relation to the contract-holder, or a member of the contract-holder's family who, at the time the care was provided, lived with the contract-holder – s.77(1)(c) and (4);

d) he or she meets the basic residence condition, as set out in section 76(3) and (4), and

e) at the time of the contract-holder's death there was no other dwelling which the person was entitled to occupy as a home: s.77(4).

Again, if the contract-holder was a priority successor in relation to the occupation contract, the references in (c) above to the contract-holder include the person the contract-holder succeeded: s.77(3).

For these purposes, "carer" means a person who:

i. provides or intends to provide a substantial amount of care for another person on a regular basis, and

ii. does not provide or will not provide that care because of a contract of employment or other contract with any person: s.77(5).

A person does not provide care because of a contract merely because he or she is given board or lodging or because he or she may become qualified to succeed as a reserve successor: s.77(6).

Fixed-term standard contracts and joint contract holders – contractual right to transfer on death

By s.142, RH(W) Act 2016, if a fixed term standard contract provides that on the death of a joint contract-holder his or her rights and obligations under the contract may be transferred in the course of the administration of his or her estate then it must also provide that a transfer may not be made unless the joint contract-holder gives notice to the other joint contract-holders before his or her death that such a transfer will be made and the transferee is not entitled to occupy the dwelling without the consent of the other joint contract-holders.

Fixed-term standard contracts and sole contract holder – contractual succession permitted via administration of deceased's estate

By s.139, RH(W) Act 2016, fixed-term standard contracts with a sole contract-holder may provide that on the death of the sole contract-holder, the contract may be transferred in the course of the administration of the contract holder's estate and s.73 (right to succeed) does not apply to a fixed term standard contract that contains such provision. Section 155 of the 2016 Act (termination of contract on death) is not incorporated as a term of a fixed-term standard contract that contains such provision.

Competing successors

If there is one priority successor, that person succeeds: s.78(2). If there are two or more, they may agree between themselves who should succeed in default of which the landlord chooses: s.78(3).

If all the persons are reserve successors, the person who succeeds to the contract is (or the persons who succeed to the contract are) the person (or persons) selected by agreement between the reserve successors, or if they fail to agree (or fail to notify the landlord of an agreement) within a reasonable time, whichever of them the landlord selects.

There is a right of appeal to the County Court by an overlooked successor (whether priority or reserve) against the landlord's selection: s.78(5) and (6). Any such appeal must be brought before the end of the period of four weeks starting with the day on which the landlord notifies the person that he or she has not been selected: s.78(7). The appeal is a full merits appeal and not merely a review of whether the landlord acted lawfully in reaching its decision: s.78(8).

Points to note

- In Wales, for secure tenancies, the test for ascertaining who is a qualifying successor is reminiscent of the approach in England and Wales prior to the Localism Act 2012. However, a major change under RH(W) Act 2016 is that a spouse can succeed first and a family member or carer can succeed thereafter. Children are also excluded if they have failed to reach their majority by the time the contract holder dies.

- The local authority decides who out of competing successors succeeds but unlike in England, there is a right of appeal to the County Court for an overlooked successor.

- Standard fixed-term contracts can provide for transfer on death.

CHAPTER SEVEN

SUCCESSION AND CHILDREN UNDER 18 YEARS OLD

From 1.12.22, what follows applies only in England. In Wales, minors (children below the age of 18) cannot succeed to a tenancy: s.74(3), RH(W) Act 2016.

A child can only contract for "necessaries" where they have sufficient capacity to understand the responsibilities arising from the contract: *Gillick v West Norfolk & Wisbech Area Health Authority* [1985] UKHL 7. Accommodation is broadly considered necessary and therefore a licence agreement for the provision of accommodation is binding against a minor so long as they have capacity to contract for necessaries in the usual way.

However, "legally" (as opposed to in equity) minors (defined as those persons below the age of 18 years old) cannot hold a legal "estate in land" (remember that phrase from Chapter One; a periodic tenancy is such an estate): s.1(6) Law of Property Act 1925. If a person purports to grant a legal tenancy to a minor, the grant operates as a declaration that the grantor holds the land in trust for the minor: para 1(1)(b), Sch.1, Trusts of Land and Appointment of Trustees Act 1996.

So, at law, a child cannot be a legal tenant yet the law does not exclude a child from those persons qualifying to succeed to a tenancy. How does this work legally and practically?

The key is to recognise that whilst a child cannot hold a legal tenancy "at law", they can benefit from such a tenancy in equity. Accordingly, a child can hold a tenancy in equity: *Kingston upon Thames RLBC v Prince*

[1999] 1 F.L.R. 593. The natural consequence of a child holding a beneficial interest in a tenancy is that there must be someone in whom the legal title is vested. This is known as the trustee.

The obligations of a trustee are many and complex and covered in Snell's Equity much more fully. In broad terms however, and for present purposes, a trustee cannot put himself in a position where there is a conflict between his personal interests and his duties as trustee: *Bristol & West Building Society v Mothew (t/a Stapley & Co)* [1998] Ch. 1 CA (Civ Div).

So, where a local authority or a housing association inadvertently or mistakenly grant what is a legal tenancy to a child they become the trustee of that tenancy (see para.1, Sch.1 Trustees of Land and Appointment of Trustees Act 1996) and therefore the legal tenant. The result is that they cannot serve on themselves any notice to end the tenancy: *Alexander-David v Hammersmith and Fulham LBC* [2009] EWCA Civ 259. This poses problems for a social landlord, particularly when one has regard to a trustee's inability to terminate this type of trust until the child becomes an adult at 18: s.6(2) Trusts of Land and Appointment of Trustees Act 1996.

However, *Alexander-David* is <u>not</u> a succession case. The means by which the equitable tenancy is conveyed to a child by operation of law (i.e., as a result of automatic statutory succession and para.1, sch.2, Trusts of Land and Appointment of Trustees Act 1996) do not result in the landlord becoming the legal tenant. The legal tenancy is either vested in the personal representatives of the deceased former tenant and administered in accordance with his or her will or if the former tenant died intestate, it vests in the Public Trustee.

The combination of the automatic statutory succession provisions of the Housing Act 1985 and 1988 (post-Localism this converts contractual succession to automatic statutory succession), *Prince* and the common law rules on transmission of a tenancy on death result in the following:

- a child who succeeds on the death of the former tenant becomes the tenant in equity, not at law;

- if the tenant dies and has a will, the trustee of the tenancy will be the personal representatives of the estate in the first instance and thereafter the heir to the tenancy on administration of the estate;

- if the tenant dies intestate, the Public Trustee holds the legal title to the tenancy (which creates its own problems because the Public Trustee will not pay the rent nor be liable for any arrears – discussed below);

- The landlord can probably end the tenancy for breach of a term pertaining to rent or conduct in either circumstance (testate or intestate former tenant) albeit there is no express authority on the subject. It is unlikely any court will countenance a social tenancy subsisting (even for a child) without payment of rent or compliance with terms relating to conduct.

Where a former tenant dies intestate and the legal tenancy vests in the Public Trustee pending the taking out of letters of administration but a child succeeds to the tenancy in equity a problem is created for the social landlord. The Public Trustee is not personally liable to pay the rent for the tenancy nor is he liable for arrears: s.9(3) of the Administration of Estates Act 1925 ("[t]he vesting of real or personal estate in the Public Trustee by virtue of this section does not confer on him any beneficial interest in, or impose on him any duty, obligation or liability in respect of, the property". A similar problem occurs in respect of a personal representative or administrator of an insolvent estate – again, no personal liability arises to discharge the rent obligation. This issue was discussed in "Minor tenants: Part 2 – liability and grounds for possession" J.H.L. 2014, 17(3), 62-67, by Andrew Arden KC and Amy Knight.

The conclusion reached in that article is that neither vesting in the Public Trustee, nor the personal representative of an insolvent estate, would likely bar a claim for possession based on a breach of the terms of a tenancy agreement (albeit it is acknowledged that a court is likely to respond to the various issues discussed in that article in such a way "that maintains the secure tenancy for the minor, following the lead set in *Prince*").

The position pre-Localism (i.e., where a contractual succession may have necessitated a new grant of tenancy) or where there is a "discretionary succession" which necessitates the grant of a new tenancy, will give rise to the issues identified in *Alexander-David*. In such circumstances, social landlords have to be very careful about how the new tenancy is granted such that a separate trustee of the equitable tenancy exists. This might be done e.g., by the grant of a joint tenancy with an adult (which takes effect as the grant of the legal estate to the adult, on trust for himself and the minor: Sch.1, para.1(2), Trusts of Land and Appointment of Trustees Act 1996).

A viable alternative would be to have a declaration of trust in the tenancy agreement such that the adult to whom it is granted holds the legal tenancy on trust for the child pending the transfer of the legal title to the child on attaining the age of 18.

Points to note

- Children cannot hold estates in land (which includes tenancies) as a matter of law and so a specific device is needed in equity (a trust) to allow them to have the benefit of the tenancy.

- The trustee should not be the landlord ideally as it prevents the landlord from evicting the child if they fail to comply with the terms of the tenancy.

- In succession cases, the landlord is not at risk of becoming the trustee on the grant because there is no grant. The legal title vests in either the executors of the deceased estate or the Public Trustee pending its vesting in the administrator.

CHAPTER EIGHT

POSSESSION PROCEEDINGS

Ending the tenancy and bringing possession proceedings in order to evict an occupant who remains in the property but is not qualified to succeed is not straightforward. If not properly considered, researched and prepared early on, it can result in litigation risk and ultimately costs being paid out to the potential successor.

Broadly speaking, any claim against a failed successor will engage either a mandatory claim for possession based on termination of the tenancy by notice to quit or a claim against a person who has inherited the tenancy but cannot succeed to it by Ground 7, Schedule 2, Housing Act 1988.

Even in circumstances where a person succeeds, the property may be too big for them (under-occupied) and the landlord may want to free it up for allocation to a larger family. Possession proceedings can be brought by local authorities and private registered providers of social housing and registered social landlords in such circumstances albeit the making of a possession order is not guaranteed.

Failed succession

Tenant NTQ

In many cases, in the case of a will/executor, it is likely if there is no dispute about succession that any tenancy will simply be ended by the executor (in whom the tenancy has vested) serving notice to quit on the landlord.

This should be explored as a first step in all relevant cases.

However, if this is not or cannot be done, then the landlord must take steps to end the tenancy.

Fixed term tenancies

If the tenancy is a fixed-term tenancy, the landlord may have to activate any break clause or rely on the death of the tenant as a basis for re-entry if there is provision in the tenancy for the same.

Service of a notice to quit will be of no assistance because they apply to periodic tenancies.

How to serve notices is considered below in the context of periodic tenancies. If there is either no will or no executor to administer the estate, broadly speaking, to be effective, any notice must be copied, and that copy send to the Public Trustee's Office.

Periodic tenancies

A periodic tenancy continues after the tenant's death: *Parker d. Walker v Constable* (1769) 3 Wils. 25. Resultantly, the landlord must determine the tenancy by notice to quit before seeking possession: *Wirral BC v Smith* (1981–82) 4 H.L.R. 81 CA.

Thus, the one thing the Public Trustee can do during this period is to receive a copy of a notice to quit (necessarily from the landlord) to end the tenancy vested in him: *Epping Forest D.C. v Pomphrett* [1990] 2 E.G.L.R. 46.

Service of any notices to quit etc.

Prior to the grant of probate or of administration, at which point the executor or administrator becomes entitled to deal with the property of the deceased, the identity of the personal representatives is not known publicly.

To account for this, s.18 of the Law of Property (Miscellaneous Provisions) Act 1994 provides a method for serving notices on a tenant's estate prior to the grant of probate or administration and provides as follows:

> "(1) A notice affecting land which would have been authorised or required to be served on a person but for his death shall be sufficiently served before a grant of representation has been filed if:
>
> (a) it is addressed to 'The Personal Representatives of' the deceased (naming him) and left at or sent by post to his last known place of residence or business in the United Kingdom, and
>
> (b) a copy of it, similarly addressed, is served on the Public Trustee."

Section 19(1) of the 1994 Act empowers the Public Trustee to give directions as to the office or offices at which documents may be served on him by virtue of the substituted s.9.

The Public Trustee must keep a register recording any notices served under s.18, which must include the name of the deceased, the description of the land to which the document relates and the date on which the notice was entered on the register: reg.3, Public Trustee (Notices Affecting Land) (Title on Death) Regulations 1995 (SI 1995/1330), made under s.19, 1994 Act.

How to register the notice with the Public Trustee

The website GOV.UK advises:

"Address the written notice to: 'The Personal Representative of [full name of the tenant who died] of [last known address for the tenant who died]'.

Email the notice and NL1 form to the Public Trustee

Order a NL1 application form to register a notice from OyezStore or from Shaws. The form costs no more than £8.26.

You'll get it by post. Email a copy of the notice and a scan of your completed NL1 form to osptcontrolunit@ospt.gov.uk.

You must buy a new form for each application – you cannot use a photocopy. You can make your own version of the form, as long as it's laid out in the same way and includes all the relevant information.

Pay the application fee

It costs £40 to register the notice. You can only pay by Bacs. Transfer the fee to the following account:

Sort code	Account number	Account name
80 26 50	10014069	The Public Trustee

Include the name of the deceased in the payment reference.

Get a decision about your application

The Public Trustee will register or reject your application. You should get an email within 15 working days of the Public Trustee getting your application and payment.

> If your application is registered, you'll be told the date it was put in the register.
>
> If your application is rejected, for example because it's incomplete, you'll be told why the Public Trustee cannot register it.
>
> You can search the Public Trustee's register (by ordering a search via obtaining a Form NL2 at a cost of £8.26, emailing this to osptcontrolunit@ospt.gov.uk, and paying £20 for the search) if your notice is registered, for example to check that you can legally rent the property again or sell it."

The subsequent grant of letters of administration does not invalidate the interest of the Public Trustee retrospectively or any action to terminate that interest by notice to quit so that the administrator does not derive any title to a lease validly terminated by notice to quit before the grant of letters of administration: *Fred Long & Sons v Burgess* [1950] 1 K.B. 115.

The problem with notices to quit served on the Public Trustee

In the case of premises let as dwellings for the purposes of the Protection from Eviction Act 1977, there is a minimum period of four weeks: s.5, PEA 1977. The four-week minimum can include day of service or of expiry (but not both): *Schnabel v Allard* [1967] 1 Q.B. 627. A proper quitting date must, however, be identified, or be identifiable with reasonable certainty: *Dalgleish v Jennings* [1982] C.L.R. 268, CA. The notice must expire either at the end of a period of the tenancy or on the first day of any period: *Crate v Miller* [1947] K.B. 946.

To avoid error, most notices to quit include a saving clause. A date will be stated for when the notice is to expire but to this are added the words:

> "or at the end of the period of the tenancy expiring next [four weeks or such other applicable period] after the service of this notice upon you."

This wording complies with the requirements both of a four-week minimum period (if a dwelling) and that the notice must end on the last day of a period of the tenancy: *Hussain v Bradford Community Housing Ltd* [2009] EWCA Civ 763; [2010] H.L.R. 16. The fact that a date and a savings clause have been included does not mean the date cannot reasonably be ascertained: *Spencer v Taylor* [2013] EWCA Civ 1600; [2014] H.L.R. 9.

A person must ensure a copy of the notice was served on the Public Trustee prior to the date by which possession ought to be given up pursuant to that notice: *Gateway Housing Association v Personal Representatives of Ali & Anor* [2020] EWCA Civ 1339; [2021] 1 W.L.R. 289; [2020] E.G.L.R. 37.

Assured tenancy and Ground 7

If the tenancy becomes assured on the vesting of the tenancy in a person in occupation of the property as their only or principal home but not entitled to succeed under contract or statute, the mechanism by which possession is recovered is ***not*** by service of a notice to quit. Rather, a notice under s.8, Housing Act 1988 relying on ground 7, Sch.2 is required.

Ground 7, Schedule 2, Housing Act 1988 is a ground where a person who inherits a tenancy in circumstances where they are not entitled to succeed to it can be evicted on mandatory grounds.

By s.7(1), Housing Act 1988, the court cannot make an order for possession of a dwelling-house let on an assured tenancy except on one or more of the grounds set out in Schedule 2 to that Act. Section 7(3) of the 1988 Act goes on to state that if the court is satisfied that any of the grounds in Part I of Schedule 2 (which includes Ground 7) is established then subject to proper notice being given (and to any available defence based on the tenant's Convention rights, within the meaning of the Human Rights Act 1998) the court shall make an order for possession.

Ground 7 provides so far as material:

> "The tenancy is a periodic tenancy […] which has devolved under the […] intestacy of the former tenant and the proceedings for the recovery of possession are begun not later than twelve months after the death of the former tenant […].
>
> For the purposes of this ground, the acceptance by the landlord of rent from a new tenant after the death of the former tenant shall not be regarded as creating a new [...] tenancy, unless the landlord agrees in writing to a change (as compared with the tenancy before the death) in the amount of the rent, the period or length of term of the tenancy, the premises which are let or any other term of the tenancy."

It is noteworthy that Ground 7 does not refer to a tenancy devolving specifically on the heir/beneficiary, merely that it devolves under a will or on intestacy (which it does initially on the Public Trustee pending a grant or the taking out of letters). The position is thus different from that under the secure tenancy scheme in the Housing Act 1985 where the statute expressly provides that "[w]here there is no person qualified to succeed the tenant, the tenancy ceases to be a secure tenancy when it is vested or otherwise disposed of in the course of the administration of the tenant's estate […]" subject to certain limited exceptions: s.89(3), Housing Act 1985.

There is a tension here between when a notice to quit might be served and when a s.8 notice relying on ground 7 might be served. This tension formed the basis of argument in *Clarion v Carter* (above). Based on consideration of the authorities and the definition of "tenant" and "tenancy" in s.45, Housing Act 1988, ultimately, the court concluded that there was no equitable tenancy held by the occupant during the period between the former tenant's death and assent under a will or on intestacy (merely a form of inchoate right to call for the administration of the estate). Accordingly, the tenant condition was not satisfied in this period and assured status was lost (meaning a notice to quit might be served during this period). It is only once an assent has occurred that ground 7 becomes available because the tenancy is then held by the occupant legally.

Service of a notice under s.8, Housing Act 1988 must be in the prescribed form and served on the failed successor tenant.

Upon expiry of the notice to quit and/or the s.8 notice, the landlord must bring possession proceedings by virtue of s.3, Protection from Eviction Act 1977 in the former instance and s.7, Housing Act 1988 in the latter.

Compliance with policies

Whether acting for landlords or potential successors, after scrutinizing the tenancy agreement and the legal framework closely, one must consider any applicable policies of the landlord which apply to decision-making in the context of succession. These policies often set out how a landlord will approach determining a potential successor's entitlement to succeed in the light of the relevant statute, any contractual rights in the tenancy agreement and as a matter of discretion in (usually) exceptional circumstances. Legal advisors must then establish based on the documentary evidence (contemporaneous) and on detailed instructions whether the policy has been followed. A substantial failure to comply with policy without good reason can form the basis of a public law defence. To see such a defence in action, see the decision in *Clarion v Carter* in the High Court, referred to above.

Accordingly social landlords should ensure their succession policies are reviewed consistently with legal developments and the terms and conditions of its tenancy agreements and reflect what priorities the landlord has in terms of succession entitlement.

Defences to mandatory possession claims

In relation to both of the above causes of action for possession (termination of the contractual tenancy by notice to quit or a s.8 notice relying on ground 7), the court must make a possession order if satisfied that the statutory requirements for possession are made out. This is subject to three possible categories of defence:

a) A private law defence such as a failure to comply with the statutory requirements by e.g., serving a defective notice, or a potential successor establishing evidentially an entitlement to succeed contrary to the findings of the landlord.

b) A public law defence asserting that a public sector landlord, in taking the decision to serve notice and pursue a possession claim, has acted illegally, irrationally or procedurally unfairly. Examples include failing to have regard to any protected characteristic – such as disability – in accordance with the Equality Act 2010 (particularly the public sector equality duty in s.149 thereof), failing to follow any policy on succession without good reason, failing to have regard to relevant matters – such as exercising any residual discretion to allow a new tenancy to be granted in exceptional circumstances, having regard to irrelevant matters such as their own housing resources in a contractual succession claim (see *Clarion Housing Association v Carter*, above for such a successful defence) and/or treating a potential successor unfairly by e.g., failing to inform them of strict time limitations in the landlord's processes.

c) A defence of breach of Article 8, European Convention on Human Rights 1950 (with or without reliance on Art.14 of the same. A straightforward Art.8 defence was unsuccessful in

Thurrock BC v West [2012] EWCA Civ 1435; [2013] H.L.R. 5 where a failed successor had lived in the property for many years with his family. The principles relevant to an Art.8 defence (adumbrated in *Manchester CC v Pinnock* [2010] UKSC 45; [2011] 2 AC 104) were set out in the context of ss.79, Housing Act 1985 (succession provisions relating to secure tenancies).

a. "It is a defence to a claim by a local authority for possession of a defendant's home that the possession is not necessary in a democratic society within art.8(2), that is to say it would be disproportionate in all the circumstances.

b. The test is whether the eviction is a proportionate means of achieving a legitimate aim: *Pinnock* at [52]. The Supreme Court said there that it would prefer to express the position in that way rather than use the yardstick of confining an arguable art.8 defence to "very exceptional cases".

c. It is nevertheless clear that the threshold for establishing an arguable case that a local authority is acting disproportionately and so in breach of art.8 where repossession would otherwise be lawful is a high one and will be met in only a small proportion of cases: *Hounslow LBC v Powell* [2011] UKSC 8; [2011] 2 A.C. 186 at [35] (Lord Hope). The circumstances will have to be exceptional to substantiate an art.8 defence: Powell at [92] (Lord Phillips), Corby BC v Scott [2012] EWCA Civ 276; [2012] H.L.R. 23 at [35] (Lord Neuberger M.R.).

d. The reasons why the threshold is so high lie in the public policy and public benefit inherent in the functions of the housing authority in dealing with its housing stock, a precious and limited public resource. Local authorities, like other social landlords, hold their housing stock for the benefit of the whole community and they are best equipped, certainly better equipped than the courts, to make management decisions about the way such stock should be administered: *Pinnock* at [35].

e. That is why the fact that a local authority has a legal right to possession, aside from art.8 , and is to be assumed to be acting in accordance with its duties (in the absence of cogent evidence to the contrary), will be a strong factor in support of the proportionality of making an order for possession without the need for explanation or justification by the local authority: *Pinnock* at [53] and *Powell* at [37] (Lord Hope).

f. An art.8 defence on the grounds of lack of proportionality must be pleaded and sufficiently particularised to show that it reaches the high threshold of being seriously arguably: *Powell* at [33] and [34] (Lord Hope).

g. Unless there is some good reason not to do so, the court must at the earliest opportunity summarily consider whether the art.8 defence, as pleaded, and on the assumption that the pleaded facts relied upon are correct, reaches that threshold. If the pleaded defence does not reach that threshold, it must be struck out or dismissed. The resources of the court and of the parties should not be further expended on it.

h. Even where an art.8 defence is established, in a case where the defendant would otherwise have no legal right to remain in the property, it is difficult to imagine circumstances in which the defence could operate to give the defendant an unlimited and unconditional right to remain. That might be the effect of a simple refusal of possession without any qualification. It is particularly difficult to imagine how that could possibly be appropriate in a case where the defendant has never been a tenant or licensee of the local authority. Otherwise, the effect of the

> art.8 defence would be that the court would have assumed the local authority's function of allocating its housing stock, preferring the right of the defendant to remain, without any tenancy or contract, over all the other people entitled to rely on the local authority's statutory housing duties and without the benefit of any knowledge of who those people are and their circumstances and of other relevant matters which would properly guide the local authority in housing management decisions."

Under-occupying successor tenant

England

In England, a local authority can rely, in relation to a secure tenancy on Ground 15A, Schedule 2, Housing Act 1985 where a tenant succeeds to a tenancy the property of which is too extensive.

The ground was introduced by the Localism Act 2012 and applies where the secure tenant dies after 1 April 2012.

Ground 15A provides:

> "The dwelling-house is in England, the accommodation afforded by it is more extensive than is reasonably required by the tenant and—
>
> (a) the tenancy vested in the tenant by virtue of section 89 (succession to periodic tenancy) or 90 (devolution of term certain) in a case where the tenant was not the previous tenant's spouse or civil partner, and
>
> (b) notice of the proceedings for possession was served under section 83 (or, where no such notice was served, the proceedings for possession were begun) more than

six months but less than twelve months after the relevant date.

For this purpose "the relevant date" is—

(a) the date of the previous tenant's death, or

(b) if the court so directs, the date on which, in the opinion of the court, the landlord (or, in the case of joint landlords, any one of them) became aware of the previous tenant's death.

The matters to be taken into account by the court in determining whether it is reasonable to make an order on this ground include—

(a) the age of the tenant,

(b) the period (if any) during which the tenant has occupied the dwelling-house as the tenant's only or principal home, and

(c) any financial or other support given by the tenant to the previous tenant."

There is no specific equivalent to this ground in the Housing Act 1988 because Ground 9, Schedule 2 provides that a possession order can be made if

a) suitable alternative accommodation is available for the tenant or will be available for him when the order for possession takes effect; and

b) the court considers it reasonable to make an order.

When assessing reasonableness, all relevant circumstances existing at the time of the possession claim must be taken into account (including whether other occupants have subsequently moved in such that the property is no longer under-occupied).

Also, the court must have regard specifically to those matters prescribed by Part III, Schedule 2, Housing Act 1988 relating to suitability, namely:

- a certificate of the local housing authority for the district in which the dwelling-house in question is situated, certifying that the authority will provide suitable alternative accommodation for the tenant by a date specified in the certificate, shall be conclusive evidence that suitable alternative accommodation will be available for him by that date.

- Where no such certificate as is mentioned in paragraph I above is produced to the court, accommodation shall be deemed to be suitable for the purposes of Ground 9 above if it consists of either

    - premises which are to be let as a separate dwelling such that they will then be let on an assured tenancy, other than a tenancy in respect of which notice is given not later than the beginning of the tenancy that possession might be recovered on any of Grounds 1 to 5 above, or an assured shorthold tenancy, within the meaning of Chapter II of Part I of this Act, or

    - premises to be let as a separate dwelling on terms which will, in the opinion of the court, afford to the tenant security of tenure reasonably equivalent to the security afforded by Chapter I of Part I of this Act in the case of an assured tenancy of a kind mentioned in sub-paragraph (a) above,

  and, in the opinion of the court, the accommodation fulfils the relevant conditions as defined in paragraph 3 below.

- The relevant conditions are that the accommodation is reasonably suitable to the needs of the tenant and his family as regards proximity to place of work, and either

    - similar as regards rental and extent to the accommodation afforded by dwelling-houses provided in the neighbourhood by any local housing authority for persons whose needs as regards extent are, in the opinion of the court, similar to those of the tenant and of his family; or

    - reasonably suitable to the means of the tenant and to the needs of the tenant and his family as regards extent and character; and

    - that if any furniture was provided for use under the assured tenancy in question, furniture is provided for use in the accommodation which is either similar to that so provided or is reasonably suitable to the needs of the tenant and his family.

- Accommodation shall not be deemed to be suitable to the needs of the tenant and his family if the result of their occupation of the accommodation would be that it would be an overcrowded dwelling-house for the purposes of Part X of the Housing Act 1985.

Each member of the tenant's family who lives in the property with the tenant has a potential interest in possession proceedings and is entitled to be joined as a party to those proceedings: *Wandsworth London Borough Council v Fadayomi* [1987] 3 All E.R. 474, [1987] 1 W.L.R. 1473, CA. This does not mean that a landlord must issue against each such family member, rather that if the family member wishes to be joined, they can apply to the court and will ordinarily be permitted to do so.

There is nothing to prevent (in appropriate circumstances) the court from making a possession order if satisfied that as yet unidentified accommodation having particular characteristics would be reasonably suitable to meet the needs of the tenant and his family, and that such accommodation will become available. The court has jurisdiction to make a possession order which would not take effect until such accommodation has in fact become available ('a conditional order for possession'): *Reading Borough Council v Holt* [2013] EWCA Civ 641, [2013] H.L.R. 536.

A successor in respect of property A who has a possession order made against them under Ground 15A retains any accumulated time for the purposes of the right to buy when being relocated to other suitable accommodation: *Manchester City Council v Benjamin* [2009] 1 All ER 798.

Wales

In Wales, Ground 16, Housing Act 1985 previously applied until 1 December 2022.

Since then, a Welsh social landlord can recover possession in reliance upon s.155, RH(W) Act 2016 (termination of tenancy where sole tenant dies and there is no qualified successor) which provides:

> "(1) If the sole contract-holder under an occupation contract dies, the contract ends
>
> > (a) one month after the death of the contract-holder, or
> >
> > (b) if earlier, when the landlord is given notice of the death by the authorised persons.
>
> (2) The authorised persons are
>
> > (a) the contract-holder's personal representatives, or

(b) the permitted occupiers of the dwelling aged 18 and over (if any) acting together.

(3) The contract does not end if under section 74 one or more persons are qualified to succeed the contract-holder.

(4) The contract does not end if, at the contract-holder's death, a family property order has effect which requires the contract-holder to transfer the contract to another person.

(5) If, after the contract-holder's death, the family property order ceases to have effect and there is no person qualified to succeed the contract-holder, the contract ends

(a) when the order ceases to have effect, or

(b) if later, at the time the contract would end under subsection (1).

(6) This section is a fundamental provision which is incorporated as a term of all occupation contracts, except fixed-term standard contracts that contain the provision mentioned in section 139(1) (transfer on death of sole contract holder); section 20 provides that this section

(a) must be incorporated, and

(b) must not be incorporated with modifications."

This section appears in Part 9, Chapter 2 entitled "Certain circumstances in which occupation contracts can end without a possession claim". Accordingly, it seems that a landlord in Wales can now take back possession of such a property where there has been a failed succession. It will be interesting to see whether this approach proves workable.

By contrast, in Wales, the equivalent of Ground 15A (under-occupation) is found in Schedule 8, Ground G (reserve successors and provides:

> "The contract-holder succeeded to the occupation contract under section 73 as a reserve successor (see sections 76 and 77), and the accommodation comprised in the dwelling is more extensive than is reasonably required by the contract-holder."

This ground requires a court order under ss.160 and 210, RH(W) Act 2016 (estate management grounds). The court may not make such an order for possession on this ground unless:

a) Ground G in Schedule 8 is satisfied,

b) it considers it reasonable to do so, and

c) it is satisfied that suitable alternative accommodation is (or will be) available to the contract holder.

Reasonableness

Reasonableness in relation to this ground is to be determined in accordance with RH(W)A 2016, Sch 10 and what amounts to suitable alternative accommodation is to be determined in accordance with RH(W)A 2016, Sch 11.

Schedule 10 provides that the court, in determining whether it is reasonable to make such an order must (amongst other things) have regard to the following circumstances to the extent that the court considers them relevant (and to the extent that it is not otherwise required to have regard to those matters; for example, under the Human Rights Act 1998:

Circumstances as regards the contract-holder

- The probable effect of the order or decision on the contract-holder (and on any permitted occupiers of the dwelling).
- If the case is one in which the court may decide to postpone the giving up of possession, the likelihood that the contract-holder will comply with any terms that may be imposed.

Circumstances as regards the landlord

- The probable effect of not making the order, or of the decision, on the landlord's interests, including the landlord's financial interests.
- If the landlord is a community landlord, the probable effect of not making the order, or of the decision, on the landlord's ability to fulfil its housing functions, including assisting other persons in need of accommodation.

Circumstances as regards other persons

- The probable effect of the order or decision on
    - contract-holders and permitted occupiers of other dwellings of the landlord,
    - persons who have asked the landlord to provide them with housing accommodation, and
    - persons living, visiting or otherwise engaging in a lawful activity in the locality (and persons who wish to live, visit or engage in lawful activities in the locality).
- If a possession claim is made on the ground in section 157 (breach of contract), the probable effect of the circumstances set out in paragraph 10 on the persons mentioned in sub-paragraph (1).

New occupation contract offered

- Whether the landlord has offered or undertakes to offer a new occupation contract (whether for the same dwelling or other dwellings) to one or more of the persons occupying or living in the dwelling.

Circumstances relating to estate management Ground G

- If the landlord makes a possession claim relying wholly or partly on estate management Ground G (accommodation not required by reserve successor)
    - the age of the contract-holder who succeeded to the contract under section 73,
    - the period during which the contract-holder has occupied the dwelling as his or her only or principal home, and
    - any financial or other support given by the contract-holder to the contract-holder who died (or, if the contract-holder who died was the successor of an earlier contract-holder, to that earlier contract-holder).

The court cannot however have regard to the likelihood that a person will be assisted under Part 2 of the Housing (Wales) Act 2014 or Part 7 of the Housing Act 1996 (homelessness) is not a relevant circumstance (subject to any requirement to have regard to that circumstance to which the court is subject): Schedule 10, paragraph 14, RH(W) Act 2016.

These statutorily prescribed relevant circumstances are unlikely to be exclusive of any other relevant circumstances.

Suitability of alternative accommodation

Schedule 11 contains the characteristics by which suitability is determined:

Estate management grounds: certificate of local housing authority

- where the landlord under the secure contract is not a local housing authority, a certificate of the local housing authority for the area in which the existing dwelling is situated, certifying that the authority will provide suitable alternative accommodation for the contract-holder by a date specified in the certificate, is conclusive evidence that suitable alternative accommodation will be available for him or her by that date.

Suitable accommodation

- In the absence of such a certificate or where the landlord is a local housing authority, accommodation is suitable if
    - it is to be occupied by the contract-holder under an occupation contract that gives him or her security of occupation reasonably equivalent to that given by the existing contract, and
    - in the opinion of the court it is reasonably suitable to the needs of the contract-holder and his or her family (which must be determined in accordance with paragraph 4).
- If the existing contract relates to a separate dwelling, accommodation is not suitable unless it is a separate dwelling.

Needs of contract-holder and his or her family

- The court must determine whether accommodation is reasonably suitable in relation to the needs of the contract-holder and his or her family in accordance with this paragraph.
    - The court must consider (among other things)

  - the needs of the contract-holder and his or her family as regards extent of accommodation,
  - if the landlord is a private landlord, the needs of the contract-holder and his or her family as regards character of accommodation,
  - the means of the contract-holder and his or her family,
  - if the contract-holder or a member of his or her family works or is being educated, the distance of the accommodation from the place (or places) of work or education,
  - if proximity to the home of any member of the contract-holder's family is essential to the well-being of the contract-holder or that member of his or her family, the proximity of the accommodation to that home,
  - the terms of the existing contract and the terms of the occupation contract under which the accommodation is to be occupied, and
  - if furniture was provided by the landlord under the existing contract, whether furniture is to be provided for use by the contract-holder and his or her family and, if so, the nature of that furniture.

- If the landlord is a community landlord, the court must also consider the nature of the accommodation which it is the practice of the landlord to allocate to persons with similar needs.

Overcrowding

- Accommodation is not suitable to the needs of the contract-holder and his or her family if, as a result of their occupation of the accommodation, the accommodation would constitute an overcrowded dwelling for the purposes of Part 10 of the Housing Act 1985.

It should be borne in mind that where a person is moved from an under-occupied property and granted what amounts to a new tenancy of less extensive accommodation, the fact of that succession follows the tenant and there will be no further succession to a tenancy of the smaller property.

Issuing a claim for possession

Once the time limits for notice have expired in England and the tenancy has been determined in Wales, the landlord can issue possession proceedings under Sections I (England) and IV (Wales) of Part 55, Civil Procedure Rules 1999 (as amended): https://www.justice.gov.uk/courts/procedure-rules/civil/rules/part55, and the Practice Direction 55A: https://www.justice.gov.uk/courts/procedure-rules/civil/rules/part55/pd_part55a.

Points of note

- There are two types of possession claim which arise in the context of succession: (i) evicting a person who does not qualify to succeed and (ii) evicting a person who is under-occupying accommodation to which they have succeeded.
- Where a tenant does not qualify to succeed, the tenancy ceases to have any statutory protection and is terminable by notice to quit.
- Where a tenant succeeds to a property too extensive for his needs, a social landlord can take possession proceedings and a court may make an order if it considers it reasonable and there is suitable alternative accommodation made available.
- Defences can be either to the strict legal entitlement to seek possession (e.g., failing to serve proper notice, reasonableness, suitability where relevant) or it can be based on a public law challenge and/or failure to observe Art.8, ECHR 1950.

CONCLUSION

Succession law is complicated for all concerned. The key to tackling any issue arising in context is to establish the type of tenancy you are dealing with (which may not always be apparent on the face of the agreement), be familiar with the governing legislation and know the terms of the tenancy agreement relating to succession inside out.

With an appreciation of the complexity of the area (hopefully!) conveyed by the foregoing chapters, I cannot stress highly enough the importance of lay persons taking some legal advice (initially from your Citizens Advice Bureau, Shelter or other local advice agency – if you have one). In a society where housing in the private sector is increasingly unaffordable, the existence or not of succession rights is significantly valuable, both to landlords and tenants.

MORE BOOKS BY LAW BRIEF PUBLISHING

A selection of our other titles available now:-

'A Practical Guide to Parental Alienation in Private and Public Law Children Cases' by Sam King QC & Frankie Shama
'Contested Heritage – Removing Art from Land and Historic Buildings' by Richard Harwood QC, Catherine Dobson, David Sawtell
'The Limits of Separate Legal Personality: When Those Running a Company Can Be Held Personally Liable for Losses Caused to Third Parties Outside of the Company' by Dr Mike Wilkinson
'A Practical Guide to Transgender Law' by Robin Moira White & Nicola Newbegin
'Artificial Intelligence – The Practical Legal Issues (2nd Edition)' by John Buyers
'A Practical Guide to Residential Freehold Conveyancing' by Lorraine Richardson
'A Practical Guide to Pensions on Divorce for Lawyers' by Bryan Scant
'A Practical Guide to Challenging Sham Marriage Allegations in Immigration Law' by Priya Solanki
'A Practical Guide to Legal Rights in Scotland' by Sarah-Jane Macdonald
'A Practical Guide to New Build Conveyancing' by Paul Sams & Rebecca East
'A Practical Guide to Defending Barristers in Disciplinary Cases' by Marc Beaumont
'A Practical Guide to Inherited Wealth on Divorce' by Hayley Trim
'A Practical Guide to Practice Direction 12J and Domestic Abuse in Private Law Children Proceedings' by Rebecca Cross & Malvika Jaganmohan
'A Practical Guide to Confiscation and Restraint' by Narita Bahra QC, John Carl Townsend, David Winch
'A Practical Guide to the Law of Forests in Scotland' by Philip Buchan
'A Practical Guide to Health and Medical Cases in Immigration Law' by Rebecca Chapman & Miranda Butler
'A Practical Guide to Bad Character Evidence for Criminal Practitioners by Aparna Rao
'A Practical Guide to Extradition Law post-Brexit' by Myles Grandison et al

'A Practical Guide to Hoarding and Mental Health for Housing Lawyers' by Rachel Coyle

'A Practical Guide to Psychiatric Claims in Personal Injury – 2nd Edition' by Liam Ryan

'Stephens on Contractual Indemnities' by Richard Stephens

'A Practical Guide to the EU Succession Regulation' by Richard Frimston

'A Practical Guide to Solicitor and Client Costs – 2nd Edition' by Robin Dunne

'Constructive Dismissal – Practice Pointers and Principles' by Benjimin Burgher

'A Practical Guide to Religion and Belief Discrimination Claims in the Workplace' by Kashif Ali

'A Practical Guide to the Law of Medical Treatment Decisions' by Ben Troke

'Fundamental Dishonesty and QOCS in Personal Injury Proceedings: Law and Practice' by Jake Rowley

'A Practical Guide to the Law in Relation to School Exclusions' by Charlotte Hadfield & Alice de Coverley

'A Practical Guide to Divorce for the Silver Separators' by Karin Walker

'The Right to be Forgotten – The Law and Practical Issues' by Melissa Stock

'A Practical Guide to Planning Law and Rights of Way in National Parks, the Broads and AONBs' by James Maurici QC, James Neill et al

'A Practical Guide to Election Law' by Tom Tabori

'A Practical Guide to the Law in Relation to Surrogacy' by Andrew Powell

'A Practical Guide to Claims Arising from Fatal Accidents – 2nd Edition' by James Patience

'A Practical Guide to the Ownership of Employee Inventions – From Entitlement to Compensation' by James Tumbridge & Ashley Roughton

'A Practical Guide to Asbestos Claims' by Jonathan Owen & Gareth McAloon

'A Practical Guide to Stamp Duty Land Tax in England and Northern Ireland' by Suzanne O'Hara

'A Practical Guide to the Law of Farming Partnerships' by Philip Whitcomb

'Covid-19, Homeworking and the Law – The Essential Guide to Employment and GDPR Issues' by Forbes Solicitors

'Covid-19 and Criminal Law – The Essential Guide' by Ramya Nagesh

'Covid-19 and Family Law in England and Wales – The Essential Guide' by Safda Mahmood

'A Practical Guide to the Law of Unlawful Eviction and Harassment – 2nd Edition' by Stephanie Lovegrove
'Covid-19, Brexit and the Law of Commercial Leases – The Essential Guide' by Mark Shelton
'A Practical Guide to Costs in Personal Injury Claims – 2nd Edition' by Matthew Hoe
'A Practical Guide to the General Data Protection Regulation (GDPR) – 2nd Edition' by Keith Markham
'Ellis on Credit Hire – Sixth Edition' by Aidan Ellis & Tim Kevan
'A Practical Guide to Working with Litigants in Person and McKenzie Friends in Family Cases' by Stuart Barlow
'Protecting Unregistered Brands: A Practical Guide to the Law of Passing Off' by Lorna Brazell
'A Practical Guide to Secondary Liability and Joint Enterprise Post-Jogee' by Joanne Cecil & James Mehigan
'A Practical Guide to the Pre-Action RTA Claims Protocol for Personal Injury Lawyers' by Antonia Ford
'A Practical Guide to Neighbour Disputes and the Law' by Alexander Walsh
'A Practical Guide to Forfeiture of Leases' by Mark Shelton
'A Practical Guide to Coercive Control for Legal Practitioners and Victims' by Rachel Horman
'A Practical Guide to Rights Over Airspace and Subsoil' by Daniel Gatty
'Tackling Disclosure in the Criminal Courts – A Practitioner's Guide' by Narita Bahra QC & Don Ramble
'A Practical Guide to the Law of Driverless Cars – Second Edition' by Alex Glassbrook, Emma Northey & Scarlett Milligan
'A Practical Guide to TOLATA Claims' by Greg Williams
'A Practical Guide to Elderly Law – 2nd Edition' by Justin Patten
'A Practical Guide to Responding to Housing Disrepair and Unfitness Claims' by Iain Wightwick
'A Practical Guide to the Construction and Rectification of Wills and Trust Instruments' by Edward Hewitt
'A Practical Guide to the Law of Bullying and Harassment in the Workplace' by Philip Hyland
'How to Be a Freelance Solicitor: A Practical Guide to the SRA-Regulated Freelance Solicitor Model' by Paul Bennett

'A Practical Guide to Prison Injury Claims' by Malcolm Johnson
'A Practical Guide to the Small Claims Track - 2nd Edition' by Dominic Bright
'A Practical Guide to Advising Clients at the Police Station' by Colin Stephen McKeown-Beaumont
'A Practical Guide to Antisocial Behaviour Injunctions' by Iain Wightwick
'Practical Mediation: A Guide for Mediators, Advocates, Advisers, Lawyers, and Students in Civil, Commercial, Business, Property, Workplace, and Employment Cases' by Jonathan Dingle with John Sephton
'The Mini-Pupillage Workbook' by David Boyle
'A Practical Guide to Crofting Law' by Brian Inkster
'A Practical Guide to Spousal Maintenance' by Liz Cowell
'A Practical Guide to the Law of Domain Names and Cybersquatting' by Andrew Clemson
'A Practical Guide to the Law of Gender Pay Gap Reporting' by Harini Iyengar
'A Practical Guide to the Rights of Grandparents in Children Proceedings' by Stuart Barlow
'NHS Whistleblowing and the Law' by Joseph England
'Employment Law and the Gig Economy' by Nigel Mackay & Annie Powell
'A Practical Guide to Noise Induced Hearing Loss (NIHL) Claims' by Andrew Mckie, Ian Skeate, Gareth McAloon
'An Introduction to Beauty Negligence Claims – A Practical Guide for the Personal Injury Practitioner' by Greg Almond
'Intercompany Agreements for Transfer Pricing Compliance' by Paul Sutton
'Zen and the Art of Mediation' by Martin Plowman
'A Practical Guide to the SRA Principles, Individual and Law Firm Codes of Conduct 2019 – What Every Law Firm Needs to Know' by Paul Bennett
'A Practical Guide to Adoption for Family Lawyers' by Graham Pegg
'A Practical Guide to Industrial Disease Claims' by Andrew Mckie & Ian Skeate
'A Practical Guide to Redundancy' by Philip Hyland
'A Practical Guide to Vicarious Liability' by Mariel Irvine
'A Practical Guide to Applications for Landlord's Consent and Variation of Leases' by Mark Shelton
'A Practical Guide to Relief from Sanctions Post-Mitchell and Denton' by Peter Causton

'A Practical Guide to Equity Release for Advisors' by Paul Sams
'A Practical Guide to Financial Services Claims' by Chris Hegarty
'The Law of Houses in Multiple Occupation: A Practical Guide to HMO Proceedings' by Julian Hunt
'Occupiers, Highways and Defective Premises Claims: A Practical Guide Post-Jackson – 2nd Edition' by Andrew Mckie
'A Practical Guide to Financial Ombudsman Service Claims' by Adam Temple & Robert Scrivenor
'A Practical Guide to Advising Schools on Employment Law' by Jonathan Holden
'A Practical Guide to Running Housing Disrepair and Cavity Wall Claims: 2nd Edition' by Andrew Mckie & Ian Skeate
'A Practical Guide to Holiday Sickness Claims – 2nd Edition' by Andrew Mckie & Ian Skeate
'Arguments and Tactics for Personal Injury and Clinical Negligence Claims' by Dorian Williams
'A Practical Guide to Drone Law' by Rufus Ballaster, Andrew Firman, Eleanor Clot
'A Practical Guide to Compliance for Personal Injury Firms Working With Claims Management Companies' by Paul Bennett
'RTA Allegations of Fraud in a Post-Jackson Era: The Handbook – 2nd Edition' by Andrew Mckie
'RTA Personal Injury Claims: A Practical Guide Post-Jackson' by Andrew Mckie
'On Experts: CPR35 for Lawyers and Experts' by David Boyle
'An Introduction to Personal Injury Law' by David Boyle

These books and more are available to order online direct from the publisher at www.lawbriefpublishing.com, where you can also read free sample chapters. For any queries, contact us on 0844 587 2383 or mail@lawbriefpublishing.com.

Our books are also usually in stock at www.amazon.co.uk with free next day delivery for Prime members, and at good legal bookshops such as Wildy & Sons.

We are regularly launching new books in our series of practical day-to-day practitioners' guides. Visit our website and join our free newsletter to be kept informed and to receive special offers, free chapters, etc.

You can also follow us on Twitter at www.twitter.com/lawbriefpub.

www.ingramcontent.com/pod-product-compliance
Lightning Source LLC
LaVergne TN
LVHW022303200926
848481LV00004B/1199

9781914608377